AF342205

DIVINE COMEDY

Divine Comedy

INSTALLATION AND ESSAY

Eric Cameron

NATIONAL GALLERY OF CANADA
Ottawa, 1990

Published in conjunction with the exhibition **Eric Cameron: Divine Comedy** organized by the National Gallery of Canada and presented in Ottawa from 5 January to 25 February 1990, and by the Winnipeg Art Gallery and in Winnipeg from 17 March to 29 April 1990.

Canadian Cataloguing in Publication Data

Cameron, Eric, 1935-
Divine comedy. —

Text by Eric Cameron.
Issued also in French under title: Divine comédie.
ISBN 0-88884-594-4

1. Cameron, Eric, 1935-   —Exhibitions.
I. National Gallery of Canada.   II. Title.

N6549 C35 A35 1989   709.2   CIP 89-099506-0

Design: Associés Libres, Montréal
Printing: M.O.M. Printing

PRINTED IN CANADA

Available from your local bookseller or
The Bookstore
National Gallery of Canada
380 Sussex Drive, Box 427, Station A
Ottawa   K1N 9N4

For Gregory, Edwin, and Matilda

To Justify the Ways of God to Men

William Blake, slightly misquoting John Milton

To justify the inevitability of its particular forms

Eric Cameron, quoting Clement Greenberg out of context

Contents

Preface

The writings in this book, like the works in the installation it accompanies, record stages in a process of growth. "Oedipus and Sol LeWitt" was written initially for a lecture given at the Ontario College of Art in January 1986. It was never my intention that it should find its way into print as I then wrote it, and yet, even though I have become acutely conscious of ambiguities and inconsistencies and of ideas to which I no longer hold, my many attempts to revise it have always left me feeling that more had been lost than was gained. It appears here with only modest revisions of wording for the sake of clarity and accessibility.

"12. What I Want To Do — " (which appears here essentially without alteration) was written some months earlier in connection with an application for a Canada Council Project Cost grant. Question 12 asked the applicant to state what he or she wanted to do. I seized the opportunity, there and then, to do something I had wanted to do for some time: record as much as I could remember about the circumstances surrounding the production of each of my Thick Paintings. In some places there are repetitions of the material contained earlier in *Bent Axis Approach* and later in "Oedipus and Sol LeWitt," but this is of the essence. These writings are, after all, the product of the mind that moves the hand that continues to make the Thick Paintings. I venture to predict the next reformulation (which may be entitled "Inevitability/Justify/Forms/Particular/of its/the/to") will also contain repetitions, which will again be just as essential a component of my changing patterns of thought.

Eric Cameron

Oedipus and Sol LeWitt

1. Eric Cameron, *Bent Axis Approach* (Calgary: The Nickle Arts Museum, 1984).

My theme is the pursuit of conviction. When I gave the title *Bent Axis Approach* to my installation at the Nickle Arts Museum in Calgary in 1984 and to the book[1] that accompanied it, one of the things I had in mind was that the task of locating conviction in art may best, perhaps, not be approached directly. The issues of art's nature and function have been addressed too often already. If no one else has ever been able to produce conclusive arguments, how can we even begin to take the task seriously? When I told my first-year class we were going to spend the afternoon discussing the question "What is Art?" they groaned out loud.

By the time I realized conviction had better be allowed to catch us unawares, the key phrase had already presented itself. I had been rereading Clement Greenberg's "Avant-Garde and Kitsch"[2] in preparation for another discussion with that selfsame first-year class, and this one phrase kept coming back: "to justify the inevitability of its particular forms." As Greenberg used the phrase, it did not have anything to do with art at all. It was the forms of society he was talking about, not of art. When I wrote *Bent Axis Approach*, I thought it might have been the fact that Greenberg had come to be regarded as the most eminent of formalist critics that had made me want to test the applicability to art of this phrase containing his first reference to form, but I am not sure I ever felt that explanation could account for the resonance the words had for me. As I mulled them over, they seemed to indicate exactly the experience I received from those works of art I valued most highly. Moreover, the phrase seemed to embody my ambition for my own art better than any set of words of any length I had encountered anywhere else, but that is not to say I had any very clear understanding of what it might imply. It just felt right.

2. Clement Greenberg, "Avant-Garde and Kitsch," *Art and Culture* (Boston: Beacon Press, 1961), pp. 3–21.

At the time of which I am speaking, I was already well embarked on my Thick Paintings (to be continued). These date back to the spring of 1979 when, on a sunny afternoon (which may have been in late April, or perhaps early May), I began to apply coats of gesso to some objects that just happened to be available to me in my apartment: a book of matches; a telephone directory; a pair of shoes; and, in the days and weeks that followed, an apple; a beer bottle; a cup, saucer, and spoon; a paper bag; an empty S.O.S. box; an ice tray; an egg — and then another egg, when my son Edwin asked me to paint one for him; a horse-chestnut for my daughter Matilda; and a Maynard's Wine Gum box with two wine gums still in it, that had been a present from my older son Gregory; a rose; a chair; a desk lamp; two small lobsters; a mackerel; and a lettuce. Eventually, there came to be a total of twenty-seven Thick Paintings, including (in addition to the pair of shoes) a single shoe, which I painted till it was thoroughly encased in paint but haven't touched for some four or five years. The other twenty-six I continue to paint at a rate of ten thousand half-coats of paint per year. The count is in half-coats because it is necessary to let one side dry before I can turn it over and paint the other. The routine that I established within a few weeks of starting the project was to paint one side grey; let it dry; paint the other side grey; let it dry; paint one side white; let it dry; and then paint the other side white, so that after four half-coats of paint it would always be returned to the all-white condition again. What surprises me in retrospect is how casual I was in my intentions at the outset. I knew I wanted this to be a final project that I would continue for the rest of my life, but I just started one afternoon, shortly after the term was over, looking round my apartment for things to paint, and I didn't even make a note of the date, nor did I begin to keep a checklist of my work on each piece for I-am-not-quite-sure-how-many days after I started.

What seems even more strange to me now is that I did not in any way envisage in advance those occurrences that now seem to be the most important aspect of the work. I may have had some vague notion that the geometry of expanding curves should eventually cause irregularly-shaped objects to become encased in a regular sphere of paint, but that was all. In anticipation of this regular growth, I tried to brush out the paint very smoothly, and when the loop-shaped metal handle at the top of the alarm clock began to fill in quite rapidly, all I could think of was that something had gone wrong, and I tried very hard to reverse the tendency — to no avail. By the time I had reconciled myself to that distortion, a ridge had begun to appear at the edge where the half-coats overlapped, and it was growing much faster than the simple doubling of the thickness of paint in that area should give me any reason to expect. When the apple fermented in the heat of a warm early summer and blew up a great bubble on one side, it was more obvious what had happened; but at the same time, pimples were beginning to appear in a ring around its middle, even though I had tried very hard to shift the area of overlap of half-coats so as to avoid any tendency for a ridge to develop. However hard I brushed, the pimples continued to grow. Then the same sort of rash seemed to be infecting the *Beer Bottle* — but also protrusions and indentations on other pieces — and not just a single bump or blemish, but whole systems of form with their own evident consistency of rhythmical character. The shallow indentations that occurred much later on top of the *Telephone Directory* were perhaps the strangest of all. They were comparatively large and very smooth and arranged themselves in groupings accentuating the diagonals from corner to corner. I had taken especial care with this piece, brushing each coat of paint over and over, vertically, then horizontally, then vertically again, and maybe repeating the whole process several times, until each and every half-coat did look absolutely smooth. But suddenly, there they were, and at that stage, there was nothing I could do about them.

It was always the same with these new growths; they always appeared as a disruption of form, and my first response to their occurrence was always negative. But when I did make the adjustment and did accept them and did recognize their importance and did adjust my perception of the work to accommodate them, it made no difference. I found I had no more power to persuade these forms to grow than I had to prevent their growth. When a system of stud-like mounds popped up on *Newspaper*, all closely grouped in the centre, I decided I would rather have them spaced all over, but nothing I could do would persuade them to extend beyond the site they had initially claimed for themselves.

When I stopped to think about it, I realized I should not have been surprised at my inability to control completely the expanding form of my Thick Paintings. Another false anticipation I had had at the beginning was the speed at which they would grow. It turned out to be much slower than I expected. Acrylic gesso has a high water content and after the water evaporates, as I eventually realized, the resulting layer of paint might be something between one five-hundredth of an inch or one thousandth of an inch thick. On such a scale, it is inconceivable that anyone could guarantee precise evenness in each brushed-out coat of paint. The negative aspect, the fact that I could not completely control the thickness of each coat of paint, is really just common sense — or so it seems after the event, but the regularities of rhythm and form that the accumulating discrepancies present is of quite a different order of inconceivableness.

When I embarked on my final project of the Thick Paintings, I had intended not only that it should be "final" but also that it should draw together the diverse strands of my art-related activities. What I had in mind was that my writing and the various elements in my installations would be redirected to give support to the presentation of the Thick Paintings. What I now found was that they were also taking me back to the point where my art had first found its identity in the Process Paintings of fifteen and twenty years earlier. These had involved the systematic use of masking tape on rectangular canvases and, later, panels. As the system became more fully resolved around the natural logic of the process, it revealed inevitable discrepancies in the laying out of the tape which, once I had reconciled myself to the impossibility of preventing them, had slowly asserted themselves as the most significant aspect of the work, being at once the factor providing the basis of their visual complexity and consistency and the means of opening up the work to the manifestation of larger natural forces within the pattern of shapes and colours that resulted. I was amused when I found a jingle, a piece of inadvertent poetry quoted from Whewell's *Elementary Treatise on Mechanics*[3] of 1819, which suggested a scientific principle:

> And so no force, however great,/can stretch a cord, however fine,/into a horizontal line,/which is accurately straight.

The same principle that regulated the behaviour of fine cords had evidently applied also to strips of masking tape, and now, two decades later, it had found a corollary in the brushing out of fine coats of

3.   William Whewell, *Elementary Treatise on Mechanics* (1819), cited in John Bartlett, *Familiar Quotations*, 15th edition (Boston: Little, Brown and Company, 1980), p. 471. Bartlett was not the source in which I originally found this quotation. I have long since forgotten where that was.

paint.

Then as now, I had no choice but to accept and to adapt to what had taken place and what was continuing to take place. With the Thick Paintings especially, this meant more than just passively watching what happened as I worked. Almost from the first coats of paint, I had been aware that different pieces demanded to be brushed out in different ways, and as their character developed with the accumulation of successive layers, the differences became more pronounced. As new patterns of form emerged, they demanded new ways of working. Sometimes I found I had adjusted without being conscious of doing anything differently, but at other times decisions had to be thought through fully. Nonetheless, when I came to relate the notion of "to justify the inevitability of its particular forms" to my own work on the Thick Paintings, I placed the emphasis on those unsolicited unavoidablenesses of pimples, ridges, and bumps that presented an aspect of inevitability in the particular forms of each piece. This was the theme I took up when I wrote *Bent Axis Approach* in the summer of 1983, and I related those specific inevitabilities to comparably inevitable physical features in the work of Ad Reinhardt, Marcel Duchamp, and Jackson Pollock: the residual components of Ad Reinhardt's ultimately-reduced black paintings; the take-it-or-leave-it thusness of the ready-mades of Duchamp, just as they had come from the hardware store; and, most especially, the incontrovertibly drip-like forms of Pollock's dripped paint. I was aware that there was more to the work of each of those artists and I certainly hoped there was more to mine, but that was where I placed the emphasis; those were the crucial features on which the success of everything else seemed to depend.

When I reread *Bent Axis Approach* now, there is not much I would want to change, but there is more to be said. It is clear to me now that what I wrote then had to do with the particular stage my Thick Paintings had reached at that time. I had been working on them for four years and was utterly engrossed in the task. Other people might poke fun at my painting my "cabbages" (which was what people seemed to say, even though I never did paint a cabbage and never even considered painting one), but it would have been very difficult for me then to admit that I was doing anything that might be open to question. That is one point I need to address. But also, the emphasis on the physical basis needs to be qualified to a greater extent than I acknowledged at that time. Over and above both these points, there is still the tantalizing resonance of that phrase from Greenberg that needs to be accounted for.

Since writing *Bent Axis Approach* in 1983, I have pursued in my reading the ideas I broached in that essay. I have also had the benefit of many more discussions with classes and colleagues, some pieces have been shown, and there has been some critical response. On a couple of occasions I have given talks about my work, and there were questions from the audience afterwards. Meanwhile, I have continued to paint the Thick Paintings, pondering what I was about as I did so. Between times, I have lived out the daily routine of domestic life with wife, family, house and garden, and dog. One day, there was a postcard from Clement Greenberg. I had sent him a copy of *Bent Axis Approach* in acknowledgment not only of that one phrase I had borrowed out of context, but also of the way I had allowed myself to bounce quite freely off his ideas in other sections thereafter. It was an agreeable surprise when he replied, particularly as it was clear he had actually read the book.

26 December 1984

Dear Eric Cameron, Belated thanks for book, whose attention to me is flattering. But find much to argue with, especially "inevitability," which begs more than one question. But I won't argue here. You refer to my "predilection" for abstract art. Can you document that? I know it's the common notion about me, but no one, when asked, has yet been able to cite chapter and verse. Sloppy reading. My predilection, if I have one, is for literal realism *à la* Van Eyck & Canaletto & more than one 19th-cent. artist. But there are many good shots in yr. book, they gave me food for thought. I do wonder about yr. eye.

Yrs sincerely,
Clement Greenberg

What makes the pursuit of conviction so difficult, through this maze of possibilities, is that the intuition that gave me my title *Bent Axis Approach* has turned out to be right. The task of locating conviction in art cannot be approached directly. The key phrase had come from a book, but looking for conviction in books may be one of the least likely ways to find it; consciousness is too focussed to admit the sort of resonance that should direct the quest. In the event, a casual glance into a book my wife was reading turned out to be more significant than all the hours spent in the library. And when a presentation by a master of fine arts student did make a crucial contribution, enabling me to re-think the ideas I had put forward in *Bent Axis Approach*, it was strange that it should have been an illustration for a children's book, which she did not consider to be part of her art at all, that suddenly made me think of the improbable circumstances of the Oedipus plot and, at the same time, of Sol LeWitt's exhortation to follow irrational thoughts absolutely and logically.

It has been the same way with the critical responses to my work. I consider a sympathetically attuned review to be one of the great rewards of art-making, the clearly present evidence that the experience of the art has been shared. I would rank the joy of such an event as more exhilarating than the (thus far merely theoretical) prospect of a sale. It would be a happy coincidence if I could also believe that conviction had been advanced. In the case of the first article on my Thick Paintings that Cliff Eyland wrote for *Vanguard*,[4] that may have been the case, but that had more to do with the interview he recorded beforehand than with the article itself. At the time, I had no idea there would ever be an article. He was a student at the college where I was teaching, and I understood he wanted to use my comments to make an artwork of his own. Somehow that situation seemed to be conducive to the flow of thought, and I found myself articulating my ideas more clearly than I had done previously — which was very helpful to me when I came to write the book. I would very much like to be able to say the more-recent articles of Gilles Rioux in *Vie des Arts*[5] and Steven Burns in *Vanguard*[6] had advanced conviction. This last, especially, was beautifully written, witty, and well informed. He had really looked at the work and had really read the book and, moreover, had brought to its reading a philosopher's understanding of the ideas I had borrowed from philosophy. When he said of the book that "[it] surrounds the works with a sophisticated theoretical discourse ... [giving them] visual as well as intellectual richness" and of the Thick Paintings themselves that "they have a sensuousness and grandeur" and "a presence that transcends the conceptual grip on them gained from a description," it was not just the compliment that pleased, but the fact that such a writer should have made it. It would seem ungrateful if I did not

4. Cliff Eyland, "The Object of Paint," *Vanguard* (September 1983), pp. 24-25.

5. Gilles Rioux, "Thick Paintings d'Eric Cameron," *Vie des Arts*, xxx (December 1985), pp. 34-35 and 85.

6. Steven Burns, "Laying it on Thin," *Vanguard* (November 1985), pp. 15-17.

find that it had contributed something — and, of course, it has. But its immediate contribution was to reinforce commitment, to sustain the will that makes it possible to continue to work hour after hour, day after day. Burns' essay did not, on first reading, advance the quest for conviction, the guiding principle that will direct effort along the right track. Oddly enough, all three critics were more relevant to conviction in what they misunderstood. Cliff Eyland in a subsequent essay in *Arts Atlantic*[7] joined Gilles Rioux and Steven Burns in failing to recognize that what I had borrowed from Greenberg was not an idea but only a set of words. The effect of their misunderstanding was to not prompt any modification of conviction as I had already realized it in my own mind, but only to underline the need for fuller explanation so as to be able to make clear to other people what I really felt to be clear to me. It was in relation to this need that I found my reading to be proving its worth.

What Greenberg had actually written was:

> A society, as it becomes less and less able, in the course of its development, *to justify the inevitability of its particular forms*, breaks up the accepted notions upon which artists and writers must depend in large part for communication with their audiences.[8]

I will admit I had found some difficulty disentangling what this rather complex sentence was trying to say, and that may have been one of the reasons why some of the words were able to detach themselves in my consciousness and take on a new meaning. It was only when I shifted my attention to the next two sentences that the gist of it became at all clear, and then I found I did not agree with what Greenberg was saying. He continued, "It becomes difficult to assume anything. All the verities involved by religion, authority, tradition, style, are thrown into question...." When I thought of the fifth century in Athens, it seemed to me this was a period that might be described in just such terms, and yet the achievement of its art is such that it has become the classic standard by which we may still find ourselves measuring every other achievement. Moreover, when I thought of the age of Giotto and Dante and of the Renaissance period that followed, it would have been very difficult to say that society in Italy with its unstable republics, its petty despotisms, and its warring factions for pope and emperor had somehow managed "to justify the inevitability of its particular forms." I simply did not

7. Cliff Eyland, "Eric Cameron: Recent Work," *Arts Atlantic*, xix (Spring 1984), pp. 26–27.

8. Greenberg, "Avant-Garde and Kitsch," pp. 3–4.

believe what Greenberg was saying was true. I would, therefore, have to take issue with Gilles Rioux when he quotes Greenberg's sentence whole, not in any way singling out those words that had caught my attention, and says my next two chapters take their thrust from it.

Steven Burns goes further. He attempts to string Greenberg's meaning and my meaning together and make one follow logically from the other. He writes: "Greenberg's contribution, then, is his argument that in such circumstances artists cannot take the inevitable for granted. If society cannot justify its forms, art must justify its." This, however, does not represent the views of either Greenberg or myself. It is at this point that Greenberg's postcard to me becomes most helpful. When he says he "find[s] much to argue with, especially 'inevitability,'" he makes it quite plain that he can no more accept my meaning than I can accept his.

Greenberg's Marxism entailed an implicit understanding that art is contained by culture (that was why he gave the title *Art and Culture* to the collection of essays in which "Avant-Garde and Kitsch" was anthologised in 1961). Culture in turn is dependent on society. Art must draw on the energies generated by the society that produced it, and if that society has failed to keep pace with its destiny as prescribed by Marx, the resulting stagnation must also mean that art is cut off from the possibility of new input. It is inconceivable to Greenberg that art should bypass its social context and draw on larger forces not socially circumscribed. In a situation of social stagnation, Greenberg holds, art can only turn in on itself. What differentiates, for him, the art of the nineteenth and twentieth centuries in the West, when the logic of society's own stage of development pointed inevitably to communist forms, though society obstinately chose to remain capitalist, was that some artists, partially cutting themselves off from that society, had, for the first time in history, imitated the *processes of art* rather than its *effects*. In imitating the processes of art, art encountered the constraints or limits of art, but Greenberg refused to identify those constraints with those human limits by which life itself is inevitably bounded.

When I wrote *Bent Axis Approach*, I hesitated over another phrase of Greenberg's as to whether I should identify it as a found phrase. At the time, I decided there was enough common feeling, if not meaning, for me to let it stand as a direct quotation. It is clear to me now, since reading Steven Burns' essay, that I was wrong. I used Greenberg's words that "the limiting conditions of art have to be made altogether human limits" to imply that they have to speak to the human condition. In fact, Greenberg meant exactly the opposite. In its context, in the "Modernist Painting"[9] essay of 1961, it concludes his discussion of Palaeolithic painting. Greenberg holds that the cave painter "made images rather than pictures, and worked on a support whose limits could be disregarded because ... nature gave them to the artist in an unmanageable way. But the making of pictures, as against images in the flat, means the deliberate choice and creation of limits. This deliberateness is what Modernism harps on. That is, it spells out the fact that *the limiting conditions of art have to be made altogether human limits*." This is the place where I should have recognized that I was parting company with Greenberg. For him, the constraints the artist addresses are man-made limits; they are the products of culture.

It is true that in "Modernist Painting" Greenberg also refers to "real paint," but he does so in relation to the impressionist followers of Manet, and when I look at those artists' works, I find the reality of the paint is of a kind which (to quote another essay of Greenberg's) "exhausts itself in the visual sensation it produces." For my part, I have come to value the residue of natural unmanageableness in the artists' materials I use, precisely because it gives an intimation of that which is beyond cultural convention, beyond the powers of collective or individual choice, beyond perception and understanding and, of course, beyond complete control. All these terms reverse the deliberateness that Greenberg insists on. In practice, he conceives of painting as an activity relating to flat rectangular canvases. The gap between us may be gauged from my letting go of both flatness and rectangularity.

Towards the end of his essay, Steven Burns writes: "What I see here is an axis more broken than bent. Cameron may be right that the inevitabilities of our lives and our art have changed from metaphysical to merely physical ones. If so, he cannot hope for so much continuity with the Greenberg tradition." The suggestion that there was ever an axis between myself and Greenberg (and beyond Greenberg with Kant) is Steven Burns', not mine; but he is certainly right that my ideas and practice are further from Greenberg than

9. Clement Greenberg, "Modernist Painting," in *The New Art* (New York: Dutton, 1973), Gregory Battcock, editor.

I allowed in *Bent Axis Approach*. However, I think, he was wrong in suggesting that Greenberg was dealing with metaphysical inevitabilities. Earlier he writes: "What for Kant and Greenberg are *philosophical necessities*, thoughts which are true in all possible worlds, thoughts the denials of which are self-contradictions, are what Cameron does not accept." In this statement he is right about me and right — as I would expect a philosopher to be — about Kant, but I do not think he is right about Greenberg. Greenberg, from the outset, has insisted that his support of avant-garde or modernist art is not based on metaphysical absolutes or even on universal conditions within our actual world, but on its appropriateness to a particular historical situation: "There is nothing in the nature of abstract art which compels it to be so. The imperative comes from history, from the age in conjunction with a particular moment reached in a particular tradition of art."[10] Moreover, "[modern art] converts all theoretical possibilities into empirical ones."[11] Somewhere, for the early Greenberg especially, it is necessary to fit into the account the filtering through of "a superior consciousness of history"[12] and the assertion that "Capitalism in decline finds that whatever of quality it is still capable of producing becomes almost invariably a threat to its own existence."[13] Taken all together, these observations might seem to suggest that the turning of art towards the processes of art is expected to lay bare the social conditions of its production in a way that a later generation of critics might have called "deconstructive." However, drawing logical links between disconnected observations is not valid with Greenberg because the basis of his critical conclusions is not the logic of argument but the evidence of experience, which is to say, it is empirical. In "Seminar One,"[14] Greenberg refers to an observation of Kant's, and he continues: "It is not necessary here to go into the reasons Kant gave for saying this. I'd rather go into the reasons my own experience offers for agreeing with him." This seems to put Greenberg and myself back on the same side, and we are in step both in supposing the task of the artist to be empirical and in wanting to speak of the results on the basis of our own experience. What separates us is the demands we make of the experience of art. In Greenberg's earlier writing, his selections of particular artists and particular works for approval are consistently confirmed by the evidence of my own experience, but his explanations

10.   Clement Greenberg, "Towards a Newer Laocoon," *Partisan Review*, VII (Fall 1940), p. 310.

11.   Greenberg, "Modernist Painting," p. 76.

12.   Greenberg, "Avant-Garde and Kitsch," p. 4.

13.   Greenberg, "Avant-Garde and Kitsch," p. 21.

14.   Clement Greenberg, "Seminar One," *Arts Magazine* (November 1973), pp. 44–46.

(though they contain remarkable insights) are not able to account for the depths I find within that experience. My sense is that he found those too, but that there were barriers that prevented the full reporting of his experience. His entanglement with Marxism would seem to be part of the problem. Eventually, and ironically, just as his Marxism waned, his experience of art seems to have been truncated at the level of his explanations. At that point I would certainly have to break the axis.

One thing that did grate in Steven Burns' essay was his summation: "[T]here is an insistent theme in the book: the inevitabilities which constrain our existence and our arts should be faced with an attitude of humble acceptance." This is not at all what I believe either of life or of art; and I thought I had said so in *Bent Axis Approach*. If it was not sufficiently clear, some further comment is evidently called for.

What I need to stress again is that when the phrase "to justify the inevitability of its particular forms" reached out to me from the page of Clement Greenberg's essay, I accepted it as a found phrase. I recognized within the set of words the germ of an idea that could encapsulate my most deeply held (though not yet articulated) convictions about art. It seemed to me that it offered the prospect of a necessary bridge between art and life, in that the recognition of inevitability must depend on real-life experience, but that the foregrounding of that inevitability is something specific to art. You don't spend your life demonstrating the existence of brick walls, but look for a way round or find something else to do where some useful outcome can be anticipated. Humility is not required in either case. If something is inevitable, neither humility nor arrogance can make any difference. It is not a question of facing angry gods who may yet be placated by a sufficiently contrite attitude on our part. Indeed, one of my objections to Greenberg's original use of the phrase was that it brought the notion of inevitability into an area of life where I hold we should be looking for alternatives. I object to the Marxist dogmatism of the implication that a society should seek to justify the inevitability of its particular forms. I would find that sort of acceptance of the inevitable objectionable even if it were undertaken in a spirit of humility; but when we are asked to unite and struggle and even kill people in order to bring about a result that could not be otherwise, I find that horrifying.

In the lived example of my own life, the fact that I have sustained my work on the Thick Paintings should be enough to counter any suggestion of easy acquiescence to external pressures. They now require an average of about three hours work per day, weekdays and weekends, rain or shine, day in, day out, month after month, to keep me within sight of that ten thousand half-coat-per-year total. The claims of family life and of teaching responsibilities are valid claims and have to be accommodated somehow. Working out an installation, writing that book — or this one — all involve extra effort and take up more time. It needs ingenuity, as well as some resilience of will, to keep it all going. As the Thick Paintings grow larger and take longer to paint, it would seem inevitable that a limit should at some time assert itself, but I will do everything in my power to put off that inevitability as long as possible.

Within my art, my attitude is no more that of humble acceptance than it is in my life. When the desk lamp I had begun to paint yielded a gratuitous complexity that did not "justify the inevitability of its particular forms," I made a decision to remove the paint from the lamp itself and continued to paint only the cable and plug, which seemed to be fulfilling that expectation. I made a choice, just as I would in any real-life enterprise. When the mackerel I had been painting for five years (under the title of $\dot{\iota}\chi\theta\acute{\nu}s$) seemed to be losing its coherence, I first caused a ridge to be extended by deliberately laying out a thicker line of paint along a predetermined track, and then, when the result convinced me it was inauthentic, I sanded down the ridge and filled in the gap alongside with polyfilla. When I did so, I saw it was right to face up to such decisions, because they necessarily have to be faced in real life. When I said in *Bent Axis Approach* that art "inverts [the] day-to-day perspective," of such choices, what I meant was not that choices cease to be made, but that a context is established for them which focusses attention on the limiting conditions within which choice is made. When I made that choice, it carried the force of moral imperative to sustain the authentic imprint of lived experience, but that is not to claim that it was necessarily an act of free will as some existentialists would require of authentic experience. I simply have no way of knowing what external or unconscious influences may have acted on me, and within the sphere of experience, it does not matter, since I *experienced* it as a choice. It is the same way with experiential inevitability and with the experiential redefinition of eternity that I would propose. Even the laws of gravity that cause Pollock's paint to drip *down* do not apply to every time and place. We daily witness on the television screen the spectacle of astronauts floating in conditions of weightlessness. The criterion is not whether we have been informed intellectually of the possibility of alternative situations, but of how experientially the anticipation of gravity has shaped the matrix of our consciousness.

The nature of my dependency on Greenberg when I wrote *Bent Axis Approach* was that I allowed myself to bounce quite freely off what he was saying. For the most part, this means I allowed him to locate the issues I addressed. This implies a very considerable indebtedness, and I wish to acknowledge it fully, but it does not mean that I necessarily agree with Greenberg's views on any particular topic. In the process of bouncing, it did not take me long to find my way to Aristotle. Moreover, when I found the word "inevitably" used in his *Poetics*, it was not just the word but the thought that aided my quest for conviction. In Chapter 9 he writes:

> What we have said already makes it further clear that a poet's object is not to tell what actually happened but what could and would happen either probably or inevitably. The difference between a historian and a poet is not that one writes in prose and the other in verse — indeed the writings of Herodotus could be put into verse and yet would still be a kind of history, whether written in meter or not. The real difference is this, that one tells what happened and the other what might happen.[15]

It was again one particular phrase that especially caught my attention: "what could and would happen either probably or inevitably"; but on this occasion I felt that what Aristotle was actually saying about Greek tragedy more than two thousand years ago might have some bearing on the conviction I felt in relation to art and to my own art today and might help me understand why my attention had riveted on the words "to justify the inevitability of its particular forms." I felt it would be worth enquiring more precisely as to the implications of what Aristotle was saying.

It did not take me long in my reading to come across the notion of "modality," a philosophical concept my sources told me went back

15.   Aristotle, *Poetics*, translated by William Hamilton Fyfe, in same volume with Longinus, *On the Sublime*, and Demetrius, *On Style*, *The Loeb Classical Library* (Cambridge: Harvard University Press, 1932), p. 35.

to Aristotle himself, though the Greeks did not seem to have a word for it. Modality concerns what "may" be or what "must" be; possibility on the one side and necessity on the other, that depart in whichever way from what actually is. My phrase from *The Poetics* was doubly modal in that it not only speaks of "what *could* and *would* happen," and therefore deals with possibility, but also says "*probably* or *inevitably*," which is to say with statistical or absolute necessity. The library at Dalhousie University divided its classification of books on modality between "logical" and "epistemological." Those on logical modality were mostly filled with logical symbols; but I did manage to ascertain the rudimentary idea that propositions are logically possible if they are not self-contradictory and logically necessary if they are tautologous. I was reminded of Joseph Kosuth's 1968 essay "Art After Philosophy" and its statement that "... what art has in common with logic and mathematics is that it is a tautology; i.e., the 'art idea' (or work) and art are the same and can be appreciated as art without going outside the context of art for verification."[16] At the time, I had been encouraged by Kosuth's concluding assurance that "art may possibly be one endeavour that fulfils what another age might have called 'man's spiritual needs'."[17] Kosuth's own practice at that time permitted the introduction into art of such items as actual chairs, hammers, tables, sheets of glass, and neon lights, as well as photographs, texts, and photographs of texts transferred to canvas. When, however, I followed his instruction to divest these objects of their real-life associations and consider only that this is art, and art is art, I found they no longer satisfied my spiritual needs. I continued to admire one or two of Kosuth's early projects for my own reasons, but it was plain to me that logical modality was not the answer.

The books classified under "epistemological modality" quickly brought me back to Aristotle. However, what Artistotle has to say about modal concepts in the *Metaphysics* seemed to bring me up against a stumbling block. He states: "Nor can things which exist of necessity exist potentially."[18] I take that to mean that something cannot be both potential and necessary at once. When Aristotle says that the poet deals with "what could and would happen," he seems to be assigning the mode of potentiality to the poet, but when he continues with the adverbs "either probably or inevitably," he has switched to the mode of necessity, and we have just been told in

16. Joseph Kosuth, "Art After Philosophy," in *Conceptual Art* (New York: Dutton, 1972), Ursula Meyer, editor, p. 165.

17. Kosuth, "Art After Philosophy," p. 170.

18. Aristotle, *Metaphysics* (Grinnell, Iowa: The Peripatetic Press, 1966), translated by Hippocrates G. Apostle, vol. 8, p. 156.

the *Metaphysics* that something cannot be potential and necessary at the same time. This happily turned out to be a problem with the translation of the *Poetics* I was using. When I traced my fingers across the page to the original Greek, I found he did not say "either probably or inevitably" but used the phrase κατὰ τὸ εἰκὸς ἢ τὸ ἀναγκαῖον, which means literally "according to the probable or the inevitable." It becomes clear that Aristotle conceives of the "probable" and the "inevitable" as principles governing the course of events. Whatever is in accordance with these principles is deemed to be "possible" or "potential," regardless of whether or not it may ever actually have happened. The tragedian may use familiar names so as to facilitate the audience's comprehension of what is going on, but he is not concerned with the possibility of whether or not there may ever have been an actual king of Thebes called Oedipus or whether or not he figured in the events that make up Sophocles' play. He is no more concerned with these sorts of possibilities than he is with those "possible worlds" invoked by Steven Burns. I believe it is clear, however, that what Aristotle wants is not just that the events that make up the play should conform to the principles of probability or inevitability, but also that they should be presented in such a way that we experience the workings of those principles directing the action of the drama towards its tragic outcome. It is in this way that the play achieves the unity of action Aristotle was discussing in his previous chapter and also the "general truth" he will discuss in his next paragraph. In exchange for those specific verities as to the historical accuracy of the events enacted, which Aristotle asks us to relinquish, tragedy, as he conceives it, offers us an intimation of the processes governing all such situations at all times. The principles invoked here are those of human behaviour, but they might be transposed easily enough into other areas of experience. When we respond to a tragedy by Sophocles or a landscape by Constable, some pleasure may be derived from recognizing particular things, as Aristotle suggests earlier in his treatise, but the deeper response that raises the work to the level of high art is, rather, the recognition: *that is the way it is; that is how it has to be.* What we are dealing with in high art is an intimation of the inevitable state of things beyond our specific experience of the world, and we receive this intimation from the way in which a particular poem or painting or piece of music convinces us of the possibilities it raises. Not just that it convinces us intellectually of the plausibility of its plot or design, but that it engulfs us in the lived experience of the workings of inexorable law.

When I think back to the discovery of that found phrase I took out of context from Clement Greenberg, "to justify the inevitability of its particular forms," I am not able to point to any one occasion on which I suddenly realized I had found it. I may, at times, be tempted to speak of it "leaping off the page," but that was not the way it came about. I used that essay of Greenberg's every semester in my Foundation class, so I was in the habit of reading it quite frequently and I spent a lot of time discussing its implications with students. There were some pivotal sentences I had made a point of learning by heart, but other phrases, like this one, just stuck in my mind. As it kept coming back, I slowly found myself attaching more importance to it, until, eventually, I found all my ideas about art and about my own art revolving around it. Now that I come to think about how it happened, that seems to be the way I arrive at my best decisions, whether in relation to art or to my own life. Those decisions I have been happy with afterwards have usually come to me slowly. I have never been very good at making snap judgments and can remember many occasions when I have regretted quick decisions afterwards. The way I work at my Thick Paintings is consistent with the way I reach decisions best. The emergence of judgments of sensibility comes about so slowly I am often hardly aware of having come to any decision at all. I should perhaps, therefore, have been suspicious when, in the fall of 1984, I experienced a sudden flash of insight, which seemed to require the introduction of a second principle substantially modifying my slowly-won conviction.

The occasion was another discussion with students, a graduate seminar given by a master of fine arts student from France called Lorène Bourgeois. As an introduction to her work, she showed slides of illustrations for stories for children. We all thought they were very good, and I was struck particularly by the intensely human attitude of a dragon, in one illustration, lying asleep in bed. Indeed, it would have been hard to imagine any human sleeper conveying that attitude with the same poignancy. I should stress that these illustrations made no pretensions to be other than what they were: illustrations for children's stories. Nonetheless, they sparked a suspicion that high art, if it invokes the probable and the inevitable, may in some areas benefit from, and perhaps even require, that which is either impossible or highly unlikely.

When I thought back again to Aristotle's prime example, Sophocles' tragedy *Oedipus the King*, I realized that the sense of unfolding of inevitable destiny, which the play conveys, is grounded in highly improbable circumstances. How likely is it that a child staked out by its feet at birth should yet survive and mature with such physical and mental capacities as would enable it to perform the deeds attributed to Oedipus and eventually to become King of Thebes? How much strain does it place on our credulity that having been abandoned at birth he should ever again encounter his natural parents, let alone murder the one and marry the other? Is it possible that in spite of oracular warnings, someone of the astuteness of Oedipus, capable of outwitting the deadly sphinx and hence attaining the throne of Thebes, should yet encounter and kill a man old enough to be his father and then go on to marry a woman old enough to be his mother without wondering at the strangeness of the two coincidences? In a later chapter of the *Poetics*, Aristotle distinguishes between essential and accidental errors in poetry. The more serious are those that affect the persuasiveness of the representation; mistakes in relation to the subject described are excusable. "For poetic effect," Aristotle holds, "a convincing impossibility is preferable to that which is unconvincing though possible."[19] He refers twice to the Oedipus story in this connection, but offers the excuse that the improbable events occur outside the action of the play. I am still bound to wonder how a work burdened with so many contradictions of the principle of probability should yet be valued by Aristotle as the supreme example of the poet's art, if those improbabilities are, indeed, a fault. My first thought was that the implausibility of its foundation might serve to lift the play out of the realm of the actual. Degas exhorted the artist to "paint falsely and then add the accent of nature,"[20] and Picasso held that "there are no concrete or abstract forms, but only forms that are more or less convincing lies."[21] Dante described allegory as truth hidden beneath a beautiful lie.[22] And there are other instances. Moses, in Schoenberg's *Moses and Aaron*, speaks of an image "false as an image must be," at the very point where, albeit in despair,

19. Aristotle, *Poetics*, p. 25.

20. Quoted by Robert Goldwater and Marco Treves in *Artists on Art* (London: John Murray, 1976), p. 308.

21. Goldwater and Treves, *Artists on Art*, p. 417.

22. Dante Alighieri, *Il Convivio*, Treatise II, Chapter I.

he has conceded the necessity of imagery.[23] St. Augustine argued that the actor Roscius had to be a false Hecuba in order to be a true tragic actor,[24] while the image of a horse could only be true if it was a false horse. One of Oscar Wilde's characters makes a disparaging reference to "novels which are so like life that no one can possibly believe in their probability."[25]

With all the major artists of the modern movement, there is this aspect of doing something (shall we say?) improbable to such an extent that some observers have been deceived into identifying the antics as the essential import of the art. The virtually blank canvases of Ad Reinhardt, the articles Duchamp bought ready-made at the hardware store, and the pot of paint thrown in the face of the public by Jackson Pollock are not the whole story, but they are an essential part of it. With the work of each of these three artists, the specifically unusual aspects are also those which — as I attempted to demonstrate in *Bent Axis Approach* — hold the key to the inevitability of their particular forms. One of the most pleasing comments of Steven Burns with regard to my own work on the Thick Paintings was: "That I chuckled at it only deepened its poignancy." The improbability, the disruption of everyday assumptions about the way things are, is needed to accomplish the transition to a mode of experience in which the perception of things gives way to the lived experience of the inevitabilities that circumscribe their existence. In discussion at a conference a few years ago, Clement Greenberg reformulated his assessment of modernism, describing it as: "a rescue attempt, an attempt to rescue and maintain the best standards of the past ... it has been able to do so only by innovation."[26] I would like to suggest there could here be a pointer to another level of significance in the recurrent strangeness of modern art, not this time in relation to what it does for the audience, but in relation to what it enables the artist to accomplish. In his first published essay on art, Greenberg identified kitsch with the imitation of the effects of art. We may want to ask how the artist can be sure, as he judges the experiential logic of the art's unfolding, that the criterion of judgment is lived experience of the world and not the familiar patterns of other art. Removing art-practice into regions where those patterns cannot be applied might seem to hold out hope of avoiding the imitation of the effects of art. Sol LeWitt urged, "Irrational thoughts should be followed absolutely and logically."[27]

23.   Arnold Schoenberg, *Moses and Aaron*, Act II, Scene 5.

24.   St. Augustine, *Soliloquies*, Book II.

25.   "Vivian" in *The Decay of Lying*. See *The Complete Works of Oscar Wilde* (New York: Doubleday, 1923), vol. 5, p. 15.

26.   Clement Greenberg speaking in "General Panel Discussion," in *Modernism and Modernity: The Vancouver Conference Papers* (Halifax: Nova Scotia College of Art and Design, 1983), Benjamin H.D. Buchloh, Serge Guilbaut, and David Solkin, editors, p. 268.

27.   Sol LeWitt, "Sentences on Conceptual Art, 1968," in *Conceptual Art* (New York: Dutton, 1972), Ursula Meyer, editor, p. 174.

But Sol LeWitt is a somewhat sore point with me, since I had been doing work that largely fits his definition of conceptual art for the best part of a decade before he coined the term. That nobody noticed is not, of course, Sol LeWitt's fault.

What I would fault him with is an overemphasis on thought (which is perhaps why he deserves to be called a conceptual artist, while I — for all the similarities of method — do not). The tradition of high art, as I perceive it, entails a higher intimation of the real. This must start from the reality of lived experience, but must remove it from the realm of the actual. The common notion of distancing is misleading, as the example of that kind of romantic art that looks at things from a long way off, or relocates itself in a distant time or place, can testify only too persuasively. What is required, rather, is a shift that prevents our taking the reality for granted and demands that it be justified through the experience of its conformity to inevitable laws. What remains to be clarified is the nature of those laws, of that inevitability; and this brings me to my second point: that the emphasis on the physical basis of my Thick Paintings needs to be qualified to a greater extent than I acknowledged in *Bent Axis Approach*.

The translation of Aristotle's *Poetics* I have been using makes him say in the sentence immediately following the comparison of poetry and history that I have already quoted: "For this reason, poetry is something more *scientific* and serious than history, because poetry tends to give general truths while history gives particular facts." However, the word that gets translated "scientific" is φιλοσοφώτερον, which at least sounds more like "philosophical" than scientific. The distinction may not have been very significant for the Greeks, whose philosophy embraced the beginnings of science, most eminently in the practice of Aristotle himself; but it is necessary for us to enquire as to the realm in which those general truths and that inevitability are grounded. Equally, when Aristotle continues: "By a 'general truth' I mean the sort of thing that a certain type of man will do or say either probably or inevitably," it would hardly make sense for the Greeks to ask whether the man's behaviour would be found truthfully depicted according to the scientific understanding of psychology, or according to the lived experience of the dramatist, or yet again, according to some mystically transcendent view of the reality of human personality. The question would make no sense then, partly because of the limited state of the development of the behavioural sciences at that time, but also, I suspect, because it would not arouse any suspicion that each might lead to different conclusions.

For us, in the twentieth century, the situation is not at all the same. The store of knowledge is so vast and the picture of the world presented by science so bewildering and so rapidly changing that, of necessity, we find ourselves obliged to set it somewhat apart from that world of day-to-day activity in which we live our lives. Unlike the belief systems of earlier ages, science does not provide us with fixed certainties about reality beyond our everydayness. Most of us probably accept, in general, the authority of science and scientific method, but if they impinge on our lived experience, it is only to separate us from the world and from ourselves. It is not so much that we doubt the truthfulness of the constantly revised and refor-mulated pictures painted by science, confusing though they may sometimes be, any more than we doubt that representation we make to ourselves of the world in which we live from day to day. But if the world as it transcendently, unknowably, really is, can sustain such irreconcilable perspectives, we feel that it must in itself be utterly incomprehensible.

The sphere of poetry and art is and always has been that of lived experience, and lived experience provides the criterion that finally counts as regards the intimation of inevitability. In this respect, music is just the same as poetry and painting. The spectacle of a grown man or woman scraping two pieces of catgut together to produce a squealing noise is just as unlikely as the circumstances of Oedipus' early life or of Pollock's dripped paint, and yet the logic that binds the notes of a Beethoven string quartet together is just as inexorable. Only, in the case of instrumental music, it is less easy to avoid the fact that the final test is that of experience. This was something on which I laid too little stress in *Bent Axis Approach*, and yet the value to myself of that phrase I took out of context from Greenberg, "to justify the inevitability of its particular forms," may have been precisely as an instruction to my own sensibility.

Sensibility cannot be forced, any more than conviction, but must be allowed to manifest itself in its own good time and in its own way. However, I do believe that if we make aesthetic decisions long enough with a particular idea in mind (which must of necessity be clear and simple), we can have some bearing on the habitual judgments of sensibility. One of the advantages of my own practice, with its endless repetitions of the same procedures, is not only that it provides for the rehearsal of those manual operations that constantly bring each work into being again and again, but also that it allows for the slow adjustment of sensibility to accomplish the task of justification. As I look back at slides of my Thick Paintings in their earlier states, I believe there has been some progress in this direction.

In *Bent Axis Approach*, I expressed the hope that my Thick Paintings would not just register as a diagrammatic illustration of a procedural concept, but would "come to epitomize a mode of being in the world." Cliff Eyland, in the first critical response to my book, which actually appeared in *Arts Atlantic* before the publication of the book itself, took me to task as regards the notion of epitomes. It is evident I need to explain more clearly how I might look for that epitomization to come about and state the grounds on which its validity might be defended. This requires primarily, I think, that I should explain my criterion of "authentic" experience in the earlier account. As I have already indicated, I am aware of the currency of this term in existentialist writings, but my intention is very different. The separation proposed by Martin Heidegger between everyday inauthentic experience and that specifically human experience that can encompass the possibility of its own extinction in death is a notion that holds out certain temptations for me. When I decided the Thick Paintings were to be a final project, I meant that even though I might sell individual pieces I would continue the project, replacing the sold ones with new ones for the rest of my life. In practice, I decided I would do so only while death remained an indefinite certainty. I would not continue until my failing powers caused the brush to drop from my enfeebled hand. That would burden the work with a sort of pathos I would not find acceptable. If there ever comes a time when, in Auden's phrase, I "know to the [hour] when death shall cut [me] short," my intention is to bring all the Thick Paintings to the all-white state immediately and cease further work on them. In the meantime, every brushstroke is referenced to the ultimate con-straint on experience, the fact of my own mortality. But this is not my criterion of authenticity. Much less is authenticity for me that striving to assert some freedom of will that causes the heroes of Sartre and Camus to behave in such undesirable ways. On the contrary, I would wish to express the attitude and the feeling that the experience of living in the world has imprinted upon me so indelibly that it comes through when I am not aware of taking up any position at all or being subject to any emotion at all. Socially-oriented critics tell us we cannot escape the social and historical conditions of our time. I am glad to have their reassurance on this point. I would wish my experience of those things to find authentic expression in my art and I believe this can best be achieved by simply allowing these conditions to manifest their impact on my consciousness, not by introducing opinions on family life, the status of women, or American involvement in Nicaragua.

Equally, I believe I can best concentrate my lived experience of the limits and constraints of human life by allowing the residue of those concerns that have become a part of what I am to manifest even when I am not specifically intending to address those issues at all. The objects from which I started, the accumulating incrustation of paint, and its mysterious systems of irregular growth, are givens to be dealt with as I work. If I allow myself to respond indifferently, I know that what appears to be indifferent to me is not a judgment of universal validity, but something conditioned by my experience of the world. My method, applying layer after layer of paint, is conducive to this state of disinterested concentration. As I allow the inevitability of its particular forms to manifest itself in each piece, I am aware that what seems to me the neutral response in my brushing out of paint, only appears neutral to me because I have been conditioned by the world to draw the base-line of experience at that point.

Asserting the primacy of the sphere of sensibility is not to deny the significance of those aspects of art and poetry and music that enter into the sphere of believed knowledge or into the sphere of actuality. Instrumental music may have borne the stamp of the inevitabilities of its age almost completely within the sphere of sensibility, but painting and poetry in the past always set lived experience in relation to the belief systems of their time. Herodotus, as much as Sophocles, accepted the validity of oracular predictions, though Aristotle grounded the inevitability of Sophocles' art on his grasp of the workings of human nature. For Dante, it was the Christian faith that provided the larger context against which the inevitable conclusions of lived experience were drawn. In Leonardo's *Last Supper*, painted as the Middle Ages gave way to the Renaissance, science, in its early stages, merged with faith to reinforce the framework of experience of the inevitable. As science became more complex and faith waned, and belief systems failed to provide a handle on the real, the artist — and to a certain extent the composer of music — reoriented experience towards the given reality of mediums. Music is capable of doing this because its medium is the sounds that vibrate in the air we breath. Schoenberg, at the pinnacle of his achievement, benefitted from the imposition of a system of "twelve tones related only to each other," which required sensibility to adapt to the intrusion of such consonances and dissonances as the nature of those sounds yielded. Poetry is less easily directed toward this new orientation. Its medium, language — as Greenberg pointed out — is psychological, and this seems necessarily to imply a continuing overlap of the sphere of sensibility with that of believed knowledge — to however fragmentary or unsystematic a condition that belief may have been reduced. The visual artist works with the stuff of the earth and may encounter its mysteries directly. If I am right that the sensibility of the twentieth century has been shaped by the impossibility of forming a stable world picture, as I argued in that interview with Cliff Eyland and also in *Bent Axis Approach*, then it would seem to enhance the authenticity of imprinted experience if a modification of world expectations (on however modest a scale) were to take place in the course of the distillation of that experience into art. This, after the event, is the way I have always come to feel about the disruptive systems of form that have introduced themselves into my Thick Paintings as I worked.

The brief account I have just given will be seen to have built on a characteristically Greenbergian antithesis. The reorientation of the arts away from the imitation of the world and towards their own media is one of the earliest and most enduring themes in Greenberg's writing. In *Bent Axis Approach*, I described it as "one of the key insights into the art of our century." However, it is necessary that I should now point out the limitations of Greenberg's own exposition.

In "Modernist Painting," which contains the most refined statement of the antithesis in relation to the visual arts, he introduced it with the observation: "The arts could save themselves only by demonstrating that the kind of experience they provided was valuable in its own right. . . ." My criticism is that his subsequent analysis does not fulfil that promise. When he goes on to speak of the shift of emphasis from the depicted space of subject matter to the flat reality of paints and canvas, he has correctly described what took place, but he stops short there, having dealt only with the means or method by which the experience "valuable in its own right" was to be attained; he does not address the experience itself. In my account, I have attempted to penetrate beyond the point where Greenberg stopped short, but it leaves me still with the feeling of having not yet grasped the essential substance of the antithesis.

Thus far, when I have been able to pinpoint the stimuli that have directed the unfolding of conviction, whether it be Lorène Bourgeois' graduate seminar, the comments of Steven Burns, or that postcard from Clement Greenberg, they related to the professional context of my teaching and art-making activity. An instance of comparable importance occurred at home. My wife had been studying *Paradise Lost* for an English course she was taking two or three years ago, and I picked up her copy and opened the book at the beginning. Milton had never been a poet of any great significance for me, and as I read again after a lapse of many years the opening lines of that poem, the experience did not, to be frank, occasion any great conversion. Indeed, as I read it yet again now, there is something about even the key section that raises feelings of aversion and causes me to sympathize with T.S. Eliot's long-standing difficulties with that poet's art. When Milton calls on his heavenly Holy Spirit muse to "Illumine [what in me is dark] ... That to the highth of this great argument / I may assert Eternal Providence / *And justify the ways of God to men*," it is not the final line in its own context that illuminates for me the significance of that borrowed phrase of Greenberg's, but the fact that it sent me back to William Blake's slightly altered use of it as the epigraph of his own poem *Milton*. Blake had had an enormous attraction for me in my late teens, and I persevered with this very difficult poem for a long time, finding myself deeply moved,

but never quite being able to disentangle what he literally wanted
to say. What was clear was that, for Blake, the experience of art
was religious experience, affirming that we live our eternal lives in
our imaginations. I find myself uncertain as to exactly what that might
mean, whether the imagination was to be that part of personality
that would survive bodily death, or that through the experience of
art we could attain an intimation of reality beyond mortal limits.
In fact, I think *he* meant the former, but *I* would want to mean the
latter.

In the epigraph of *Milton*, the phrase from the beginning of
Paradise Lost, with the "And" changed to "To," stands alone: "To
justify the ways of God to men." That, I realised, was the other side
of the antithesis. "To justify the ways of God to men" has been the
objective of painting as much as of poetry in the past, in ages of
faith, when reality was given absolutely in revelation, just as it is
now "to justify the inevitability of its particular forms."

"To justify the ways of God to men" and "to justify the
inevitability of its particular forms" amount in the end to very much
the same thing, the one relating to an age of faith, the other to an
age without faith. Faith, in return for subservience to the divine will,
gives back to the faithful their place and prospects in an ordered
universe. When the order of things is given absolutely in revelation,
the role of the artist is that of mediator, and the work of art is perceived
and experienced in that way. In a world without faith, and especially
one like our own, whose vastness and complexity leave us incapable
of feeling certain of anything, the experience of art must begin with
the work of art itself, but it does not and must not stop there. In
the contemplation of the inevitabilities justified in aesthetic unity,
we achieve an orientation of experience, an adjustment of the observing
self to whatever the larger reality may be that encompasses it and
us.

Construed in this way, each phrase seeks to reconcile us to
the ways a higher power or larger force impinges upon and ultimately
engulfs and supersedes the objects of experience in the world. The
realization induced by science, that the myths of traditional religions
are unlikely to have the cosmic significance attributed to them, does
not immediately remove the element of mystery from the existence
of things or of ourselves. It rather shifts it to a different plane. When

Steven Burns attributes to me the idea that "the inevitabilities of our lives and our art have changed from metaphysical to merely physical ones," it is his word "merely," that I would quarrel with. There is an innuendo behind this "merely" that the higher values we cherished in the past have somehow been invalidated, whereas they have simply been shown to have emerged from different sources. There is an echo perhaps of a dualism latent in Western thought since Plato and more conspicuous under Christianity, in spite of attempts to suppress it as heresy. The physical world is deemed to be not only less real than the spiritual but also ethically negative, evil. When Marx inverted the pure spirituality of Hegel's system, the ethical connotations of spirituality were not reinvested in his materialism. The sphere of the material remained negative; conflict continued. In Volume 1 of *Capital*, he envisages the initiation of the labour process. He writes, "[Man] *opposes* himself to nature as one of her own forces."[28] Another translation says "confronts,"[29] but the attitude of antagonism is unmistakable in either case, and in this negativity Marx is only symptomatic of his age. As we distance ourselves from the initial shock of an altered world view, it should become clear that if we can conceive the possibility of anything worthy in ourselves, in our actions, in our experience, that thing of value must have been a potentiality in the material world of which we are created, and that the material therefore becomes an object of venerable attention as the source from which all experience springs.

When we do turn our attention towards the material world in that way, however, we find that we cannot penetrate its substance but can only know its forms. Natural science may have made us suspicious of the metaphysical reasons Kant gave for asserting the inaccessibility of what he calls the "supra-sensible substrate," but behavioural science gives us other reasons to agree with him and Marx and Freud and Heidegger that the world our consciousness inhabits is a representation constructed on the basis of what we are and how we can perceive and which fragments we encounter. T.S. Eliot felt the privacy of his external sensations enclosing him like a prison.[30] His response was a return to Christianity, but this entails a leap of faith, a return to otherworldliness, which becomes increasingly difficult. There are circumstances, however, when within the sphere of our own experience we receive an intimation of the

28. Maynard Solomon, editor, *Marxism and Art* (Detroit: Wayne State, 1979), p. 22.

29. Karl Marx, *Capital*, translated by Ben Fawkes (New York: Vintage Books, 1976), vol. 1, p. 283.

30. T.S. Eliot, *The Waste Land*, line 414.

"otherness" of the world of which we are a part — when we perceive discrepancies that require a modification, however minute, of the representation we have made of it to ourselves. Our first impulse, in response to the urgencies of the day-to-day living of our lives, is to resist something that may upset the pattern. I recall, on both occasions that I have shown *Lettuce* at A Space in Toronto, that visitors, after examining the system of protrusions and indentations that had developed with the accumulation of layers of paint and then hearing what the object was, would say: "Yes, I can still see the texture of the lettuce on the surface." I then explained that when I started painting it, the lettuce was enclosed in a piece of wax paper and a rubber band, just as it had come from Sobey's supermarket. If anything of the texture of the original object had survived through a thousand or two thousand coats of paint, it should have been that of the wax paper and rubber band. Another defensive response is that the occurrence of these unforeseen developments of form would be very valuable information to pass on to the paint manufacturer, who might then take steps to make the paint spread more smoothly. What interests me, however, is not any scientific understanding or theoretical explanation of how the unavoidable forms I encounter come about, but the fact that something "other" enters into my representation of the world. If I shared Eliot's view of the world, I might have felt a breach had been made in the prison wall. What this demonstrates is that the world itself is not confined by the prison of our perceptions. Wittgenstein, towards the end of the *Tractatus*, states: "It is not how things are in the world that is mystical; but *that* it exists."[31] What I believe I experienced in the progress of my Thick Paintings is an intimation of the "itness" of the existence of the world, and that intimation is mystical, albeit of a material nature: a material mysticism. Albert Einstein wrote: "The most beautiful thing we can experience is the mysterious. . . . To know that which is impenetrable to us really exists. . . . This knowledge, this feeling, is at the centre of true religiousness."[32]

Implicit in the exhortation "to justify the inevitability of its particular forms" is something that is more explicit in the Milton/ Blake parallel. Justification implies justifying to someone. It implies a particular perspective within which the revelation of inevitability has to be made meaningful. The chapter of Aristotle's *Poetics*

31. Ludwig Wittgenstein, *Tractatus logico-philosophicus*, vi:44.

32. Albert Einstein, *The World as I See It*, quoted in *Space and Time* (Pretoria: University of South Africa, 1958), E.A. Ruch, p. 39.

immediately preceding that in which he speaks of "what could or would happen either probably or inevitably" deals with the need for unity, the need to shape a work of poetic writing into a coherent entity that can be assimilated within human experience. I do not believe it is a coincidence that "Unity and Inevitability" turns out to be the heading of the culminating section of Heinrich Wölfflin's study of the High Renaissance, *Classic Art.* In practice, unity and inevitability are mutually dependent and inextricably conjoined in the experience of high art. But there has to be more entailed in unity than the achievement of a visually lucid outline. The work must present a wholeness that meets us in the fullness of our humanity, and to that end the artist must give authentically of his or her humanity in the process of its making. I was pleased that Steven Burns raised this aspect in his punning references to my name (Eric/Cire; sans cire/ without wax/sincere). But the much briefer treatment of the Thick Paintings by Diana Nemiroff in her essay of two years earlier in the *Visions* book focussed more especially on that aspect:

> Yet it seems that when the subjective element is most vigorously suppressed, it has a way of creeping in through the back door. Cameron's paintings are not pictures but objects, and it is precisely as objects that they take on a presence which has undertones of anthropomorphism ... The mirror now has lost its transparency. Its representations are deformations, giving us back the image not of ourselves but of our desires.[33]

I will admit that it took me some time to grasp the significance of her comments, which did not at all follow the direction of my own thoughts at that time. More recently, her observations have become increasingly valuable in helping me to articulate my understanding of authenticity. The most authentically expressive art of our century, the virtually blank, black paintings of Ad Reinhardt, the readymades of Duchamp, and the thrown paint of Jackson Pollock, are produced by methods that would seem to preclude the possibility of any expression at all. There is, of course, more at stake in their work than the circuitous rediscovery of subjectivity, and I hope there is in mine. Yet her text is suggestive of the development of my work that led up to the Thick Paintings, in a more precise way than I believe Diana Nemiroff knew.

Between the Process Paintings of the sixties and early seventies

33. Diana Nemiroff, "Rethinking the Object," in *Visions: Contemporary Art in Canada* (Vancouver: Douglas and McIntyre, 1983), Robert Bringhurst et al., editors, pp. 203–05.

and the inception of the Thick Paintings in '79, there were other works that strove after the subjective element, and in some of my videotapes that I would rather be allowed to forget, desire took the form of an overt sexuality. In retrospect, the most significant may have been an exercise in repression through editing entitled *Keeping Marlene out of the Picture*. But there was certainly a more rigorously repressive intention to put all that behind me when I committed myself to my final project, and it may have been for this reason that it took me some time to respond to Diana Nemiroff's interpretation. As I think of it now, if some of the desire of that middle period work has somehow managed to infuse itself into the Thick Paintings, I would be pleased, both that the work of those middle years should find a place in the developing logic of my oeuvre, but also that the new work should assimilate the animal basis of my humanity. In a question after my talk at Dalhousie Art Gallery, Steven Horne wanted to know about the original objects at the core of my Thick Paintings: are they fetishes that I spend my time constantly stroking with a brush? I would be disinclined to place so much emphasis on the original object, but when I think of the amount of physical contact, of handling and fondling my Thick Paintings receive in my daily schedule of work on them, as well as the feelings of concern that have grown through the years, of caring and cherishing, there certainly seems every reason to envisage the possibility of some such intimate investment of subjectivity as Diana Nemiroff and Steven Horne, in their different ways, have suggested. However, unless Diana Nemiroff meant something much larger by "subjectivity" and by "desire" than I can honestly convince myself she did, her response, pleasing though it is in that one aspect, attests to less than I believe high art should aspire to.

Aristotle, in the pivotal opening sentence of the *Metaphysics*, asserts that "all people *desire* to *know*." In the hierarchy of desires, the pinnacle, I believe, beyond the self-actualization proposed by Abraham Maslow, is that "other"-realization that attains to an intimation of the existences of things beyond the subjective veil of our sensory perceptions. But that otherness can only be fully realized (its inevitability fully justified) if it is known to us in the fullness of ourselves. As people may desire the highest levels of knowledge as well as the satisfaction of appetites, so knowledge in its fullness must encompass the carnal as well as the mystical beyond the intellectual. On both sides, desire and the world that mystically is, take us beyond the sphere that is given to conscious awareness, where we enact our lived experience. Freud called the source from which desire springs "id" or "it," by which he wished to convey that the impulses of lived experience emerge out of the physical basis of personality in the stuff of the material world. The circle closes, and itness is seen to circumscribe our lives. Once accepted, that mystical reconciliation with itness carries no promise of an afterlife or any of the other all-too-personal inducements of traditional religions; it is a question only of semantics if we should call that itness God.

Appendix

"12. What I Want To Do — "

— is to continue to paint my Thick Paintings (to be continued); also to pursue related activities through which their meaning may be more fully realized.

It is now more than six years* since the afternoon in late April (or perhaps early May) 1979 that I began to apply layers of paint to several objects that just happened to be available to me in my apartment. From the outset, I intended it to be a final project, and I also intended it to be a central focus around which the diverse strands of my art-related activities would be drawn together. That meant giving the Thick Paintings a central emphasis in my installations, subordinating prints, video, sound, mirrors, and such other devices as a pot of lawn grass, that I had been including for several years. But it also meant that I would cease my critical writing about other artists and re-direct that aspect of my activity towards a theoretical study of the implications of my own creative work on the Thick Paintings. Eventually, in the installation and text I am planning now, *Divine Comedy*, it might be said to have drawn in even my activities as a teacher, since that exhibit will hinge on a simulated lecture situation.**

During the period of more than six years since I started work on the Thick Paintings, so much has changed that it becomes increasingly difficult for me to envisage the state of mind in which I embarked on the venture. The development of installation strategies is perhaps the most obvious aspect. At first, it was simply a matter of giving the Thick Paintings a prominent position among the elements I had been using and trusting to a sort of hybridization process to do the rest. As I came to grasp more clearly what was happening in the Thick Paintings, it became possible to use the installation to extend the meanings I saw emerging from them into the space of the gallery itself. *On -ing and Paint*, realized at the Norman MacKenzie Art Gallery, Regina, in 1980, and three Halifax installations from later that year may be taken to represent the former type; *Bent Axis Approach*, at the Nickle Arts Museum in 1984, and the planned *Divine Comedy* represent the more developed type.

The idea of producing pamphlets relating to my installations had occurred to me before I began work on the Thick Paintings. They were to document the installation, but I would also take advantage of particular opportunities to develop the pamphlet as an art object itself. Adaptation to installations including Thick Paintings followed readily enough, and when I produced my first theoretical text, it found its place, too, in the Regina pamphlet along with photographs from my installation at the Norman MacKenzie Art Gallery.

That pamphlet, *On -ing and Paint*, was originally intended to be a full-length treatise, comparable in scope with Leon Battista Alberti's Renaissance classic *On Painting*. In the event, five months' work collapsed into a few fragments totalling no more than eight hundred words. That was in the summer of 1980. I would not wish to sell those eight hundred words short, but they were to be the last words for me in my "conceptual" attempt to locate the meaning of art through the structure of words used about art. When I tried again three years later, I was much more absorbed in the actual stuff of paint and in the process of its manipulation. When the phrase "to justify the inevitability of its particular forms" leapt off the page of a Clement Greenberg essay, quite out of context, and provided the key to my first book-length text, I was already experiencing the inevitable power of paint to determine the character of its own forms and I had adapted to a way of working in which I provided the initiating impulse for formative forces beyond my control and unperceived (except in their effects) by me. My first mature works, my Process Paintings from the sixties, had depended on a similar yielding of complete control in favour of forms and meanings that would present themselves through my interaction with the materials of art; and I came to realize that the Thick Paintings had not only brought together the divergent strands of my art practice in the late seventies, but had also brought my current practice into meaningful relationship with the initial insight of twenty years earlier. I did not deal with the relationship of my Thick Paintings to my Process Paintings in *Bent Axis Approach*, but that will be one of the themes I will take up in my next book, *Divine Comedy*.

Recognizing the restored consistency of purpose that six years' work on the Thick Paintings has brought to a creative career of a quarter of a century does not make it any easier for me to recall the expectations I had on that sunny afternoon in 1979 when I applied the first half-coat of paint to a pair of shoes, a telephone directory, and a book of matches, waited for them to dry, and then painted the other side. Considering that I intended it to be a commitment I would sustain for the rest of my life, my best recollection is that my approach was remarkably casual. I certainly anticipated that the form of the object would be modified as one expanding surface encroached on another; I may even have had a vague idea that each piece would eventually tend to become spherical; and I expected that growth would be rapid. I recall wondering how long it would

---

* "What I Want to Do —" is presented as written in July 1985.
** As visitors to the exhibition will realize, this aspect of the planned installation was abandoned.

be until they outgrew my apartment and then stopping to look at the quart-sized bottle of gesso in my hand and realising it was nearly all water. The residue after that had dried off could hardly be expected to represent any great increase in volume. Of course, the initial transformation, as the first coat of white turned the objects into instant sculptures of themselves, was spectacular, but after that I could apply a dozen more coats and hardly notice the difference. What was more noticeable was the time it took to do it. It was to sustain my motivation in the face of almost total lack of perceptible results that I began, after several days work, to keep a record of the number of half-coats I had applied (half-coats because it was necessary to wait till one side dried before I could turn the piece over and paint the other side). It may give some indication of the mood in which I began to work that I did not bother to record the date, and I am now uncertain whether it was the last days of April or the beginning of May. The first date on the first page of my checklist is "May 8 '79," but there had been several days' work before that.

Eventually I settled on a working schedule of ten thousand half-coats per year applied to some twenty-seven objects; that total number of objects was reached by October 1981 and no additions have been made since. This means an average of 370 half-coats applied to each piece, which turned out to mean a rate of growth over smooth areas (where no special conditions applied) of perhaps a third of an inch per year. If that rate of growth was less than I could ever conceivably have imagined at the outset, the amount of paint it would take, the amount of time it would take, and the increase in weight presented surprises in quite the other direction. Nonetheless, the significant fact was undoubtedly the thinness of each coat of paint. Within a film averaging between one thousandth and one five-hundredth of an inch thick, it is to be expected that irregularities could not be eliminated altogether, and it transpired that these irregularities would not, by any means, be altogether random, so that I slowly became aware of certain kinds of transformation that could be expected under certain circumstances (I am not at all sure I have encountered all possible kinds even now). My first response to each new irregularity was to attempt to suppress it. Only as the system of lumps or ridges obstinately refused to yield to more vigorous brushing did I come to accept its inevitable presence, and only after several such instances did I come to realize that it was precisely in the encounter with such unavoidable forces taking the character of forms beyond my own control that the work encountered its deepest potential for meaning. I have described in *Bent Axis Approach* the kinds of effects I encountered most frequently. What I may have understated there was the way my sensibility adapted and the way the interaction of those external forces and my attempts to accom-modate them within objects of sensibility slowly gave to each a distinctive character only indirectly dependent on the form and identity of the object from which it had started. To compensate for the overgeneralization of the account in *Bent Axis Approach*, I will add some account of each piece individually here.

Book of Matches (Plate I)

This may have been the very first piece to be started. It was certainly the first of the smaller objects I started to paint. I remember that because it had some bearing on the way the piece was to develop. When I began my Thick Paintings in late April or early May 1979 (I do not remember the date or day of the week, but I do recall it was a sunny afternoon), my intention was to use the same brush for all of them. That was a Winsor & Newton's, Series A, No. 12. This resulted in a paint surface that looked smooth enough on the larger objects, but the brush was as wide as the book of matches itself, and so my attempts revealed an evident clumsiness from the first coat. It was because of this I decided I needed to use different sizes of brushes for different pieces. It may even have been the next day that I bought a No. 6 brush from the College store; I do not remember if I also bought a No. 8 at the same time, though these were the sizes I eventually settled on. The first record I have of the division of the (by that time) nineteen Thick Paintings into groups painted with "small," "medium," and "large" brushes is an undated list, which must have been made after I began work on the two small lobsters in the last week of May and also after I had started work on a second mackerel on May 30th (since these pieces are included on the list) and before I left for England at the end of June. If my recollection should need confirmation on this latter point, this is provided by a note on the back to the effect that I was to measure the windows of the house we were buying in the South End of Halifax, so that my wife could make curtains before we returned with our children at the end of August. Evidently she had phoned and asked me to do this, and I had scribbled "get measure windows" on the first piece of paper that came to hand. The list shows that I was painting *Book of Matches* with a small brush at that time, but by then the form of the object had already been distorted by the coats applied with the large brush.

This particular book of matches had been lying around in the kitchen of my apartment for some time. I suspect it had been left there by the person who took the apartment the previous summer while I was in England. I seem to recall it had come from a night club or bar, and there may have been some orange on the cover. In every way it was a very ordinary book of matches. I decided to paint it partly because it was available, but also because of the idea of containment of fire, which sealing it with paint implied. I had been impressed by the woven "mats" of Richards Jarden and the way he used much the same kind of matches sealed within office scotch tape. I always saw that as having an autobiographical reference to the constraints of institutional life. I wanted to incorporate that symbolic aspect within my own work as well, but I was fully conscious of a shift in the implications of the metaphor. The stuff of art imposes literal constraints on creative fire just as surely as the demands of academic life.

When I started painting the book of matches, I recall I opened it up and painted half of it lengthwise, inside and out. That meant really a very narrow area to paint with a very broad brush. I would then allow the top to flip back, forming an angle which made it possible to rest it on the unpainted side while I waited for it to dry. Before long the paint itself seemed to be having the effect of closing it up (perhaps that had something to do with the way it contracted on drying), so I just allowed it to close up again. For a long time, as I continued to paint quite carefully with the No. 6 brush, it remained a quite small, thin, rectangular block, but with a very lumpy surface. It must have grown to a size of, maybe, three and a half by two and a half inches and it may have been as much as three quarters of an inch thick when I took it and *Beer Bottle* with me to New York with thoughts of getting a show there. In any event, I only showed the work to one gallery, which was not very encouraging, but an incident at customs might almost have made the trip worthwhile. I took the two Thick Paintings to Canadian Customs at the Toronto (I think) airport, just in case I encountered problems on my return. They offered to stamp each piece, and I afterwards very much wished I had let them. The idea of that sign submerged beneath the layers of paint still very much intrigues me.

That incident may have taken place in the spring of 1981. It was in late May of that year (which would have been on my return) that I decided to use larger brushes for several pieces I had previously been painting with a No. 6 brush or, in one case, a No. 8 brush. At that time, when the then total of twenty-five pieces had accumulated more than 23,000 half-coats of paint, no less than fourteen were being painted with a No. 6 brush, but only seven with a No. 8, and as few as four with a No. 12. The ratios seemed disproportionate, and several pieces were quite large enough that use of a larger brush would seem reasonable. A further factor was that painting with the fine No. 6 brush took a disproportionately long time, so by June 15th I reduced the number of paintings in that group to six. Thirteen would now be painted with a No. 8 brush and the remaining six with a No. 12. The first piece to change was *Book of Matches*, on May 25th, and it must have been the recollection that I had started

it off with a No. 12 brush that decided me on using this size again, even though it was by far the smallest piece in that category. I think, having seen how little interest it evoked as a small piece, I decided I wanted to let its size increase more quickly, and I wanted it to lose the last vestiges of its book-of-matches shape.

Previously I had shifted the location of overlap of half-coats so as to neutralise the tendency for ridges to develop. Now, I concentrated it in the middle of the piece precisely so as to build it up there and round out the still thin, slab-like form. When a ridge had built up at the centre about equal to the length of the piece, I again shifted the area of overlap to one of the diagonal axes, so as to build it up there, and I kept changing the axis at intervals, attempting to lose any sense of the original position of the book of matches within the Thick Painting.

I think I always had a feeling with this piece of having lost contact with its form through the use of too large a brush on the first day, and it was, thereafter, very difficult to find any sense of obligation to the shape on which I was working. Consequently, my application of paint at this stage, when I was deliberately trying to build it up, became increasingly loose (I might almost say "sloppy"). Since my student days, Jackson Pollock has loomed very large in my view of art, and so when the paint on *Book of Matches* began to be applied so freely that drips would run down the sides, I thought of Pollock and the way the response of liquid paint to the force of gravity had seemed to make such an important contribution to his paintings. I even wondered for a while at the careful, restrained application of paint in my Thick Paintings generally. But the dripping form of this piece did not seem right for it. The more subtle irregularities (and unpredicted regularities) that emerged from my careful painting of the other pieces seemed so much more meaningful that I decided once again to make a change. It is strange, in a way, that the ridges, ripples, and patterns of cobblestone-like bumps that emerged from the other pieces always seemed so very significant to me, once I had overcome my initial resistance. The irregularities that emerged from the use of the large brush on *Book of Matches* and from the floods of paint that I all but threw at it later, never did. So I made up my mind, in effect, to start afresh, accepting the form as it then was and still continuing to work with a No. 12 brush, which was not, by now, any too large. I would brush out the paint as regularly as I could, endeavouring to smooth out each coat as much as the rather weird shape it had now assumed would permit, and I would continue to shift the area of overlap of half-coats so as to approximate a generally spherical form. Where there were protrusions, I would have the weight of the piece rest on these so as to flatten them down. I have now been continuing in this way for perhaps as long as three years and have every intention of continuing in the same way.

The episode with the sloppy dripping paint I have been describing represented a more serious crisis of confidence than I have, thus far, encountered with any other piece. In retrospect, I simply accept it as part of the history of the piece and continue to paint as before. One further recent development, however, remains to be recounted. In order to bring the full weight of the piece to bear on the most developed protrusions, I found it necessary to support it with wedges. These have resulted in small triangular indentations appearing all over the work. They tend to survive many applications of paint, but new ones continually appear as the old ones are smoothed over.

As of July 7th, 1985, my records show that *Book of Matches* has accumulated 3195 half-coats of paint and has a diameter of about nine inches. It has only been shown once, in *Bent Axis Approach* at the Nickle Arts Museum.

Telephone Directory (Plate II)

This piece, by comparison, has been much more straightforward. I remember quite distinctly that I began it on the first afternoon. I used the No. 12 brush then, and six years and two thousand half-coats of paint later, I am still using a No. 12 brush. I do not recall that I had any special reason for deciding to paint it, other than the fact that it was available and seemed an interesting shape to work with. In those days, the Halifax phone book had white and yellow pages combined, so it may have been rather thicker than the present yellow pages alone. I anticipated it might be difficult persuading the open edges to seal over, but that proved not to be a problem. I simply brushed paint over the edge, and after a few coats, it had congealed into a solid block. From the start, I made the overlap of half-coats come around the edge, and that might well have caused a ridge to develop there. However, this did not happen because the book was quite thick, and I was able to move the exact line of overlap up and down a little. What came as a surprise was that more-or-less vertical forms began to push out at the corners fairly soon after I started. They were quite noticeable; people commented on the fact when I showed them at A Space in 1982, but photographs I had taken at that time show the development of these corner ridges to have been very modest when compared with their growth since.

I have always tried to brush out the paint on this piece very thoroughly, using vertical and horizontal strokes over the whole surface alternately, until it is quite smooth. Using the heavy No. 12 brush, it has been possible, in this case, to prevent the emergence of the "cobblestone" protrusions that more often appear on pieces done with a No. 6 or No. 8 brush. However, during the last year or so, a rhythmical system of very slight depressions, only visible in a raking light, has begun to appear on the top surface and the underside. These seem to ripple out from the centre towards the shorter sides, extending as far as the diagonals between the corners and hence adding to the diagonal emphasis already provided by the corner protrusions.

In general, apart from the corner protrusions, the contours of *Telephone Directory* have taken on a soft, smoothly rounded form. People have described its appearance as "cushion-like," but as the rate of growth of the corner protrusions continues to accelerate, and the diagonal emphasis of the surface undulations also remains, I can envisage the possibility that this might change in time. The corner protrusions are quite different in character from each other, but they all tilt quite distinctly to the right. I can foresee that if they continue to grow and to tilt, the piece might eventually come to suggest a four-bladed propeller. But that is looking a long way into the future.

From tip of corner protrusion to tip of corner protrusion the piece has now formed a rectangle about sixteen by fifteen and a half inches, but because of the way these protrusions have developed, the axis of this rectangle has turned at ninety degrees to that of the original telephone directory. It is almost exactly four inches thick. I have shown the piece three times: at the Centre for Art Tapes in Halifax in my *Chrysalis* installation of November 1980; and together with *Lettuce* and *Cup, Saucer, and Spoon* in an installation entitled *(to be continued)* at A Space in May 1982 and again in March 1985. My intention is to ask A Space to show the same three pieces every three years.

As of July 7th, 1985, *Telephone Directory* has accumulated 2052 half-coats of paint, according to my checklist.

Pair of Shoes (Plate III)

They were a pair of brown shoes; the make was Clark's Wallabies, and they were very well worn. The soles may even have been starting to leave the uppers, but I do not recall exactly. Oddly enough, once I started to paint them, they seemed to pull back into shape, so that after a few coats you might have supposed there was a brand new pair of shoes inside my Thick Painting. This type of shoe has laces, and I painted them with the laces in, the left lace of the left shoe hanging over its left side onto the floor and making a strange sort of protrusion as the paint fixed it into position. I was rather surprised how effective the paint was in doing this — in fixing everything into position. Some difficulty might have been anticipated in joining the two shoes together, but this turned out not to be a problem. I applied paint thickly to the inside of each, pressed them together, allowed the paint to dry, and that was it.

At first the laces and the piping that Clark's Wallabies have round the front made an intricate linear pattern, but the spaces soon began to fill in as I worked, and the forms of laces have long since disappeared, though there is still just a hint of the piping. What still remains quite distinct is that protruding tip of a lace at the left, now showing as a small round form, almost like a partially submerged table-tennis ball around which a quite large saucer-like slab of paint has developed on the line of overlap of half-coats. My practice from the beginning with *Pair of Shoes* was to paint the soles and part way up the sides; then, when they had dried, turn them over and paint the upper section. That protruding piece of shoelace (which was really just an inch of metal tip) was the natural place to locate the overlap of half-coats, and in this instance, I decided just to accept the invitation it offered. But for a long time I moved the precise line of overlap a little up and down elsewhere, so the building up of a characteristic ridge did not happen so quickly. Because the back of the shoe offers more height to shift the line of overlap than the toe does, it was to be expected a ridge would develop at the front first, and this was indeed the case. I might even have been able to hold up the development of a ridge at the back longer than I did, had not the weight of the front ridge started to make the piece topple forwards while I had it upside-down on the bench to paint the soles. When I decided to allow a ridge to form at the back as a counterpoise, I set the line of overlap about halfway up, so it did not make a flat plane all round both shoes, but curved upwards towards the back. It happened, as the ridge began to extend all round, that for a length of a couple of inches very near the right heel, a double ridge formed quite spontaneously. What I mean is that the overlap did not cause a simple knife-edge to grow out there as it did elsewhere, but pushed up a protrusion with a flat edge something less than half an inch in width. As I worked, I would paint over this flat area, both when the shoes were soles-up and when they were uppers-up, whereas I would stop at the ridge in those places where it had developed into a sharp edge. That meant, of course, that the double ridge was painted twice as much as any other part of the shoes. This did not mean that this twice-painted area would develop more quickly. On the contrary, it developed much more slowly than the knife-sharp ridge elsewhere and may, therefore, have contributed to the imbalance that caused the shoes to topple forward onto the toes, until I started to use a wedge to hold them up. Eventually, a matter of weeks ago, the sharp ridge finally extended over the double ridge, but the double ridge's residue still influences the form of the piece, both because there is a lump at that point within the surrounding plate of paint, and also because the edge of that plate protrudes much less far from the shoe there than elsewhere. When it came to the inside of the shoes, I just reached into the toe as far as I could with the brush, but did not trouble about the part I could not reach.

One of the first surprises that came within a few days of beginning the Thick Paintings was that the metal loop at the top of the alarm clock showed a tendency to fill in very rapidly as I painted. Because the openings into the toes of the shoes were much larger, it took longer for the effect to become noticeable there, and by then, of course, it was not really a surprise. Eventually, the gap inside both shoes did fill in with paint, about the level of the ball of the foot, leaving the toes, presumably, hollow. It was not so very long after that that the inside of each shoe filled up with paint until the flat plane of the inner sole disappeared completely. I anticipated they would fill up the remaining cavities to the level of the top of the shoes equally quickly, but I am rather pleased this has not turned out to be the case. The open top of *Beer Bottle* had filled in very quickly indeed, producing a surface on top as level as that at the bottom. The tea cup was only comparatively slower, and even the open top of *Empty Box* has long since completely closed up. But not so *Pair of Shoes*. It must be the way I always paint the open top of the shoes, pushing the brush inside and dragging the paint out and up, until the brush strokes form a regular radiating pattern that has thus far held back a tendency for hollow forms to close in, which had previously seemed impossible to check. I will be pleased if I am able to hold back the closing in of the tops of the shoes, because they will then be the only piece with hollow forms, and I have generally tried to differentiate pieces as much as possible and also to embody the maximum possible range of kinds of formations.

From the beginning, *Pair of Shoes* has been painted with a No. 12 brush. I have shown it only once, in my *Et in Arcadia Id* installation of December 1980, at the Art Gallery of Nova Scotia. It was then shown on the floor, that is, in the place for shoes rather than on the pedestal, which would have been more usual for small sculptures.

As of Saturday, July 13th, 1985, *Pair of Shoes* has accumulated some 1765 half-coats of paint and measures nineteen and a half inches long, just under nineteen inches across, and just over seven inches high.

Alarm Clock (Plate IV)

It is perhaps appropriate that I can recall more precisely the time I began this piece than in the case of most others. It was early evening of the same day I had begun work on the Thick Paintings in the afternoon. It was perhaps appropriate, too, that I should include a clock, since the incorporation of time into the spatial art of painting was so important an aspect of the project on which I was embarking. My selection of objects was generally made with half an eye to their symbolic potentialities, though I was much more concerned with allusions to the "elements," "dimensions," or "principles" of real-life experience than to any self-referential comment on the project itself. In this instance, the idea of painting a machine was also in my mind, and I liked the idea of potential movement still locked up inside the painting. On two or three occasions later, I shook it and could still get a few ticks out of it, but I did not do this too often because I wanted to preserve the potentiality for the mechanism to become operative at some later stage, and I wanted to preserve this potentiality indefinitely. Of course, there is something imponderable, if not paradoxical, about this, since the only way I can tell if the spring still has the capacity to generate a few more ticks is to shake it and listen, and in doing that I may have exhausted the potentiality. I may say, I have long since ceased to ponder this question, since the paint has grown so thick I would not be able to hear the tick anyway.

It was a very small, red alarm clock with brass fittings and black letters on a white dial. Applying the first coat of paint brought about even more of a transformation than with most other pieces, since a pair of shoes or a book of matches still reveal the essential characteristics of the things beneath the gesso, while even the telephone directory still continued to look like a book, but with a clock, the attention naturally focusses on the dial, and the first coat of paint over the glass eliminates that completely. The result, simultaneously, is that other connotations of the form become much more conspicuous. It was the kind of alarm clock that has two bells at the top, and the thought had occurred to me before that these looked like huge breasts overhanging the great round body of the clock. Once it was painted and the connotation of "face" ceased to be an alternative, the resemblance to some sort of Venus of Willendorf figure became much more conspicuous. That, however, was a long time ago, and as I have worked on it the form has changed.

One thing that I regretted, on that first evening when I began work on *Alarm Clock*, was that I removed a piece of rolled-up scotch tape that I used to prop up the back of the clock when the rear foot came off. It had three feet originally, two brass ones on either side at the front and a small piece of enamelled metal of the same kind that was used elsewhere on the body of the clock, bent over to form a support at the rear centre. Without that foot it would stand up, but precariously; and since, before I started to paint, I discarded, as an "impurity," the piece of scotch tape with which

I had replaced it, the balance of the Thick Painting would also be precarious. As I try to recall what was in my mind at the time, I think I may not have intended, at first, that the *Alarm Clock* should stand vertically. However, I soon realized that most other pieces would lie flat, and it then became much more important to me to stabilize this piece in the vertical position. I decided to attempt to create what I have called a double ridge in relation to *Pair of Shoes* — though I should perhaps not use this term here, as I was not aware, at this time, of the way ridges would form at the line of junction of half-coats. What I decided to do in practice was to paint the underneath section both when I was painting the front and when I was painting the back. In that way I could expect the doubled thickness of paint to build up a base on which the piece would stand. When, after several months, this base showed signs of developing irregularly, I would stick on split peas to fill in the gaps. I found these would rapidly take on a form very similar to that which naturally grew out of the process of painting itself. They proved an inconspicuous way of making adjustments, and I have continued to use them to fill in gaps whenever the base develops in such a way that it would not rest evenly in the upright position. (In fact, I keep this piece lying down on back or face while I work on it in my basement studio, but my intention is to exhibit it in the upright position). I added several split peas to the base of *Alarm Clock* as recently as a couple of weeks ago, but I have decided not to use this means of making adjustments with any other piece.

Alarm Clock was the first piece to reveal those particular form-generating properties of my process of painting, which has now come to seem to me the most significant aspect of the work. It is difficult for me to believe now that I did not anticipate when I started that each piece would not simply increase in size at an even rate, as I applied well-brushed-out coats of paint of apparently uniform thickness. The first indication came within no more than two or three days, when the brass loop above the two bells on my alarm clock revealed a tendency for a ridge of paint to develop inwards towards the centre, threatening to fill it in much more quickly than might have been expected. My first impulse, as with almost all the unpredicted forms that have emerged in my Thick Paintings, was to resist. But trying to paint more carefully inside the loop, so as not to leave a thicker deposit of paint there, was evidently ineffective. Within a few more days, it was clear that a ridge was also building up rather more slowly in the area of overlap of half-coats on the outside of the loop, and this eventually sharpened into a single knife-like form, which slowly spread all round the alarm clock except for the base, where I continued to make the half-coats overlap. At the sides and top, the ridge spread out comparatively rapidly, and as it grew, the original form of the alarm clock was slowly submerged within it. The space underneath the bells filled up with paint quite rapidly, and not long after that their forms began to yield to a more general shape, in which a large, quite regular ridge fanned out from the growing central mass.

At this stage, the allusion to breasts and belly was also lost; but I have been very surprised that several people recently have observed the resemblance of the developing rotundity to a plump backside. My mother-in-law thought it looked like one of the fat ladies who used to be such a common feature of postcards at sea-side resorts (I seem to have seen less of them recently). I was amused that this transformation from breasts to buttocks should have oc-curred; but I know better than to speculate on whether any un-conscious motivation on my part could have helped it along. I am certain it was not conscious, and if it was unconscious, it would follow I would be unaware of it. My way of working — accumulating very thin layers of paint in which irregularities of thickness are imperceptible — is one that would seem likely to be susceptible to unconscious psychological forces, and these might be expected to include unconscious forces within myself as well as (equally unconscious) forces generated by the physical interaction of brush and paint. Unlike the surrealists and abstract expressionists, I find those forces generated by physical interaction much more significant artistically than psychological forces; but I still find quirks of resemblance add interest, even if they are just amusing coincidences. (Someone else thought it looked like a knife blade.)

I began painting *Alarm Clock* with a No. 6 brush, but on June 28th, 1981, I changed to a No. 8 after 849 half-coats had been recorded. Whereas *Telephone Directory* and *Pair of Shoes* have always been painted lying flat on the bench, I have always held *Alarm Clock* in my hand. *Book of Matches* was at first held between forefinger and thumb but has now become so heavy it has to remain on the bench. Weight is becoming an increasing problem with *Alarm Clock*. I paint it crouching on the floor (as with every other piece) but holding it in my left hand and supporting the weight on my left knee. I always have the base towards me and I paint with generally vertical brushstrokes, though I allow them to radiate out from the base and curve round the central bulbous core of the piece to a certain extent. In my sequence of working, I always paint this piece immediately before *Brushstroke*, which is very similar in form, though that piece is meant to rest horizontally. I differentiate the treatment of the two pieces by keeping the brushstrokes on *Brushstroke* straight and parallel.

Alarm Clock, according to my records, has now accumulated 2379 half-coats of paint, as of July 15th, 1985. It measures fifteen inches in height, fourteen and a half inches across, and just over five inches thick at the thickest point. It has, as yet, never been exhibited.

Shoe (Plate V)

The day after I started work on *Pair of Shoes*, which is to say, the day after the very first Thick Paintings were begun, I had some second thoughts about that piece. The way they were stuck together seemed artificial to me. I wished I had painted only one shoe, so I started the left shoe from another pair that were also well worn. These shoes were black; they may also have been made by Clark's, but unlike the brown pair, they had no piping round the front, although they did have thick, spongy soles. The one on the left shoe was split horizontally at the front, but after a few coats of paint it pulled together again, and as with *Pair of Shoes*, the shoe inside the Thick Painting might well have been new from all appearances.

Where different options present themselves as I work on the Thick Paintings, my inclination is to allow the alternatives to differentiate similar pieces. In this instance the option was a very simple one: to paint or not to paint. As the form of the single shoe seemed much more satisfactory to me after a week-or-so's work, I decided to refrain from painting it along with the other pieces. I would continue to paint *Pair of Shoes* in the hope of losing the sense of artificiality in the process.

In the first days, I did not keep a precise record of the application of half-coats of paint, nor was I very systematic about the sequence in which I went from one piece to another. Moreover, when I did begin to keep records, I had stopped painting *Shoe* and *Crouching Lobster*. When, therefore, I began to record accumulated totals more systematically after my return from two summer months in England in September 1979, the lack of information on these two pieces was total. I did not know how many half-coats of paint I had applied to either or whether I had applied more to one than the other. With the remaining pieces, which I had continued to paint, the lack of information was only partial, and I realised that whatever the missing figure might be, it would eventually come to represent only a very tiny fraction of the total accumulation in a period of five or ten years — so I just ignored the earlier work and counted only the half-coats I had recorded. With *Shoe* and *Crouching Lobster* this would clearly be unsatisfactory. To say they had "0" half-coats would be ridiculous, so I guessed. For *Shoe* I guessed about fifty but then made it fifty-two because fifty-two is divisible by four and would be consistent with the four half-coat cycle to which I was then working (half-grey; all grey; half-white; all white). This was not altogether logical, since I had not worked to this cycle at the outset. I only started to intersperse grey coats between the white when I realized the application of white on white did not allow me to see at all clearly which parts had been painted and which not. When once I realized this, I introduced a grey coat immediately, but I then started applying two coats of white (four half-coats) over each coat of grey, because the first coat of white left enough grey showing through that I could distinguish it quite clearly from places where I had applied two coats of white. It was only when, a little while later, I came to be aware that the partial transparency of the first white coat contributed something of importance in allowing the structure of the paint layer to express itself, that I adopted a simple alternation of grey and white.

The understanding I had at that stage was that this Thick Painting (to be continued) might still be continued, even though I happened to be withholding paint from it. However, I might not have actually added any further coats of paint had it not been for an accident that occurred on the one occasion on which I have shown this piece, in an installation entitled *Tunc Autem Facie ad Faciem ad Faciem*, at Optica Gallery in Montreal in January 1982. I wanted to have it "walking up the wall" so as to imply a dislocation of gravitational field (this seemed to me an important aspect of much twentieth-century art: Pollock, Jack Bush, Peter Campus, Duchamp's *Fountain*), so I stuck it on the wall of the gallery with double-sided adhesive strips. Unfortunately, they were not strong enough to sustain the weight, and *Shoe* fell down onto the gallery floor, cracking the paint on the toe. To repair it I added six more half-coats of paint, two at the time, and four more when the work came back from exhibition. In spite of the difficulty of being sure if I really had covered every part, all this painting was done in white. That means, of course, that the whiteness is pretty dense, giving little indication of the structure of brushwork; but then, apart from a quite surprisingly rapid growth of paint inside the toe, the paint layer is not sufficiently thick to have departed very far from the original form of the shoe, and this is brought out much more clearly in solid white. *Shoe* is, therefore, distinguished from all other pieces in two ways: that it is solid white and that only (approximately) fifty-eight half-coats of paint have been applied to it, none since January 31st, 1982. It is still, naturally enough, more or less shoe-sized.

Apple (Plate VI)

There were several reasons I decided to paint an apple. Perhaps the main reason was something that had happened several years previously in one of my classes at the University of Guelph. This was my "13-220 Painting I" class, and the semester concerned may have been the winter of 1970. The idea behind the project was that the traditional apparatus of canvas and stretchers may have an inhibiting effect on the efforts of students, because of the weight of historical achievement that attaches to the form of the easel painting. To circumvent this problem, I asked students with very little painting experience to paint on different sorts of surfaces with different connotations. In other related projects, I had them painting on pieces of studio furniture, or boxes, or planks of wood that we afterwards planted in the lawn, or on huge paper bags, which they made themselves, and which were to be large enough to contain the student himself or herself. On this occasion, I asked them to paint on a piece of fruit, replicating the original markings that were already on the fruit. The particular point of this project was that it allowed students instant confirmation if they matched the colours correctly and also required a more inventive use of the brush to simulate the texture of natural fruit. The results were very pleasing, so I took quite a lot of slides and had a large colour photograph made of an attractive grouping of painted apples, bananas, and the rest, which also included a quite indistinguishable unpainted apple that someone had just brought for lunch.

The success of the project, however, is a little beside the point, because it was its one obstinate note of failure that was in my mind when I began to paint my apple in late April or early May 1979. There had been one student, an older woman (whose name I have long forgotten), who came to class on the day everyone was to present the completed work, with an apple uniformly and immaculately painted with several layers of white acrylic gesso. She said she had done this so as to fulfill the requirement and qualify for credit, but also to demonstrate her sense of its pointlessness. I have to admit this piece caught my imagination and played its part in the genesis of the whole Thick Painting venture. That, however, was nine years later. In the meantime, I had attempted to take my project out into the real world of art in much its original form; except that now, taking up the first example from Wittgenstein's *Philosophical Investigations*, I asked five friends and neighbours (including a geography teacher, an airline pilot, a housewife, a systems analyst, and an artist) to paint 5 *Red Apples*, and I added a text of my own to complete an exhibition superbly installed by curator Chris Youngs at the Owens Art Gallery in Sackville, New Brunswick.

After that show, Chris tried to preserve the fruit in a freezer, but he jokingly referred to it as their "impermanent" collection, and eventually the five red apples had to go the way of the fruit my students had painted at the University of Guelph. I still have a slide I took of that project six weeks after the event, and the contrast of fresh fruit colouring on the withered skins was really quite remarkable. One cucumber — I allowed a liberal definition of fruit

— had liquefied and drained out almost completely. Only the white "protest" apple retained its pristine appearance because its author had kept it in her freezer. Perhaps that piece stayed in my mind because of the contrary indications of her stated objections and the care with which she had executed and preserved the piece.

This, then, was part of the background to my choice of an apple. Another part was the form of the fruit itself, whose generally spherical shape contrasted with the flatness of many other objects. A third part was the biblical tradition of the fruit of "The Fall" — or, more precisely, the Renaissance tradition of rendering the fruit of the tree of knowledge of good and evil as an apple. Following the Renaissance tradition, too, I imputed a sexual connotation to the Genesis story. It was with this in mind that I pondered, for more time than I gave to such details of other pieces, whether I should leave the stalk on. I had decided without much difficulty, on the basis of my own earlier project, that it should be a red apple (even though I prefer to eat green Granny Smiths) and I chose a fairly large, dark red apple when I looked round the shelves at Scotia Foods.

What resolved the issue of the stalk for me was the recollection of a brilliantly witty lecture with which Quentin Bell would always begin his first-year course at Leeds University. It had to do with perspective and the way children draw, and it involved his drawing a house on the chalk board. He claimed that, although he knew it indicated something psychologically terrible, he had difficulty remembering to put on a chimney. I was sure removing the stalk would be just as bad as forgetting the chimney, even though it spoilt the spherical form of the fruit, so I left it on. After a few coats of paint, the stalk stuck itself down and then rapidly disappeared into the mass of paint, so the spherical form was not permanently affected, but I have to wonder what psychological secrets that might reveal?

The lesson that fruit is perishable had been well learned by me when I began work on my gessoed apple that spring morning in 1979, but it was not practical for me to keep the apple in the freezer. I hoped to prevent the withering and eventual collapse of the fruit by applying a large number of coats of paint as quickly as possible, thus building up a skin that might retard the dehydration of the apple until its form was finally cast solid in the gesso itself. What I had not reckoned on was the possibility that changes in the apple might be more than simple evaporation due to exposure to the air.

I can claim some measure of success to the extent that the apple did not wither when I might otherwise have expected it to. Instead, a lump appeared on one side and slowly swelled up until it embraced almost half the apple by the time I left for England at the end of June, though the paint layer seemed sufficiently tough and sufficiently flexible that it showed no sign of cracking, let alone bursting. I did wonder how it would survive under the heat of the summer sun that poured into my office at the College, but as someone was taking my apartment while I was away, that was where I had to leave it.

When I returned, *Apple* was utterly transformed. It had not exploded, but the gases building up inside had evidently escaped, and it seemed that almost everything inside had gone. The skin of paint had collapsed inwards in great leathery hollows on all four sides and it had, somehow, twisted around the core slightly and also toppled over to one side. My impression was that the crumpled skin of paint now accounted for almost all of what remained. As to where and how the rest had gone, the only clue was a tiny, greenish-yellow stain in the area of that sadly submerged stalk. I did take a slide of it in this state, but there was something wrong with the light meter I used, so the slide is almost invisible. By the time I took another one, the built-up paint had transformed the character of the piece.

Apple was the first piece to reveal the development of small pimple-like forms as I worked. These occurred before I left for England and even earlier than the large lump, which I assume was due to the fermentation of the fruit itself. The pimples occurred in the area of overlap of half-coats, and I was surprised by their occurrence because I spent a very long time trying to brush out each coat of paint absolutely smoothly. I was using a No. 6 brush, which was quite small enough in relation to the size of the apple, so I saw no reason to anticipate the sort of problems that had arisen from the clumsiness of the No. 12 brush in relation to the diminutive scale of a book of matches. Nor were the pimples at all the same. They were small, discrete, and quite precise in form, but sufficiently similar to each other to indicate that some common process was at work in the production of all of them. When I first noticed them, they were really minute, and I assumed that even more meticulous brushing out of subsequent layers of paint would eradicate them, but they continued to grow despite all my efforts. When I left for England, they were sufficiently large and numerous that they were beginning to impinge on each other and were achieving a sort of organic articulation within a quite clearly defined three-quarter-inch band around the middle.

The form of the piece, when I returned after the summer, was so complex, and the re-entrant curves on all four sides were so tight, that even with the smallest brush there was no hope of achieving the regularity and smoothness of paint distribution at which I had previously aimed. As the surface grew more irregular, it became difficult to detect the further development of still more irregularities within the quite unfamiliar pattern of forms that was emerging. The result was an increasingly loose handling of paint, allowing the brush to float and roll over ripples, bumps and hollows in the surface until a sort of consistency of handling slowly revealed itself and, with it, a sort of visual coherence.

Apart from one detail, that is the end of the story, because I am still using the same small brush, and still applying paint in the same way, and still experiencing the same visual coherence in the results. The one additional detail has to do with the fact that *Apple*, when I began it, was small enough to hold in the hand while I painted it. Indeed, even though it was a large apple as apples go, it was so comparatively small and light as an object that I really had to hold it in my hand to keep it still. But holding it in the hand entails a problem in that, when I have completed the half-coat, it necessarily follows that half of the piece is covered with wet paint. How do I get the Thick Painting out of my left hand and back down onto the bench without bringing the wet part in contact with the bench and causing the paint to rub off? The answer is that I press the brush against the right upper side of the apple within the area of wet paint and simultaneously press my left thumb against the dry lower left side. Sustaining the weight of the apple momentarily between these two pressure points enables me to release the fingers of my left hand from underneath the apple and allow it to come smoothly to rest on the plastic surface of the bench. The only trace this process leaves is a smudged blob of paint in the area where the brush was pressed against the wet surface, and that can easily be brushed away once the piece is safely on the bench. I still lower other pieces to the bench in this way and still brush away the resulting blemish afterwards. With *Apple*, however, I decided several years ago to leave the mark made by the brush. Moreover, the next time I painted that side, I would return to exactly the same place again and allow the effect to compound. What happened was that paint would build up around the edge of the brush-print, producing a peculiar sort of eruption in the surface, which, once under way, would grow comparatively rapidly. After a while, I would move to a new area on each side to apply the brush and this would also be the occasion to relocate the line of overlap of half-coats, hence preventing the development of ridges. When once I had moved to a new site, the old "craters" would fairly rapidly revert in character to the general structure of brushwork, and would more slowly fill in and finally merge with the rest. This means there are now many generations of these eruptions detectable with varying degrees of distinctness around the body of the work. Since any resemblance to an apple has long since disappeared, they are the most conspicuous distinguishing feature of the piece. Sometimes, so that I can find my way back to a new site, I apply a small cross with a ball-point pen at the point where the brush is to be placed. There must be several dozen sets of these crosses, submerged beneath the surface.

Apple has now accumulated 3074 half-coats of paint and as of July 16th, 1985, is almost nine inches in diameter. At that size and weight, it is much too large to hold in the hand while I paint it, but I still continue to press the brush against a predetermined spot within the wet paint at the end of each application, even though the practice is no longer functionally justified.

It has been shown only once, in an installation entitled *(to be continued)*, at Eye Level Gallery in Halifax in January 1983, along with *Paper Bag* and *Residue Plus Penknife*.

Beer Bottle (Plate VII)

This was certainly one of the earliest pieces to be started, but my recollection is very hazy as to exactly when — nor do I have any very clear recollection of why — I chose it. The fact that it was available was evidently crucial. In retrospect, I have sometimes wished I had chosen a full bottle, because I like the idea of having liquid contained within a painting, but I did not. I did have to watch expenses and I am sure part of the reason was a desire not to be wasteful. Since then, it has often seemed incongruous to me that I should have considered the cost of a bottle of beer in choosing an object that would entail such a huge amount of time and effort to paint and such an utterly disproportionate expense on paint and brushes. This must give a further indication of my attitude at the outset, which now seems very strange to me. The only more serious consideration that may have played a part — though I cannot honestly recall that it did — was the fact that I had spent a very long time drawing bottles when I first went to King's College, Newcastle, as a student in 1953. Those bottles were wine bottles, but the fact that they were empty gave a special character to the drawing studio, around which dozens upon dozens of them were ranged in every conceivable grouping. Though I have since been grateful for the way that class disciplined my powers of perception, at the time drawing bottles — or worse still, "shapes between bottles" — for six hours and more a day often seemed a cruel drudgery; and it was made still more cruel by the orgiastic connotations of that very immoderate array of empties. It was as if our drudgery was a penance for someone else's indulgence. But how much of this was in my mind when I decided on the empty Keith's bottle, some twenty-six years later, is very difficult to say. Did I ever, consciously or unconsciously, conceive the huge task of covering it with layer upon layer of paint, day after day, week after week, and eventually year after year, as a sort of penance? My parents hardly ever drank alcohol, but I have never been aware of any feelings of guilt over my own — only occasionally excessive — consumption.

I do not remember ever having painted *Beer Bottle* with other than a No. 6 brush, which is one of my reasons for thinking I could not have started it on the first afternoon, when I used only a No. 12. I also doubt if I could have negotiated the neck of the bottle with so large a brush. That would have been bound to result in the sort of breaking up of form I had experienced with *Book of Matches*; but I remember it remaining smooth for quite a long time (though the open top did fill in quickly). The photograph on the back of my *On -ing and Paint* pamphlet shows it still quite smooth in September of 1980 under 365 half-coats of paint. Only the neck shows a tendency to a characteristic ripple, which would eventually surround the whole piece, apart from the top and bottom surfaces where it had rested while waiting for me to paint the other side.

From the start I had painted the upper half, then the lower half, even though balancing the bottle on the rim of the neck while the underside dried was quite difficult. At first I made the division between half-coats come around the middle of the body of the bottle, but I soon realized the need to shift its location up and down so as to avoid the formation of a bulge or ridge. After a while, I started slanting the line of overlap diagonally, which helped spread the area of doubling of overlapped coats even more widely and also enabled me to contrive a thickening round the neck so as to produce a larger surface at the top, which would be more stable when the piece needed to stand upside down. In the fall of 1979, when I set up my basement studio in our newly-acquired South End home, I found the balance of *Beer Bottle* still sufficiently precarious that I would rest it directly on the hard floor in the upside-down position, but then on the padded bench in the upright position. My benches consisted of two of my old Process Paintings on heavy panels supported by small piles of bricks. The movers had wrapped the paintings in styrofoam and then corrugated cardboard. I added a covering of heavy plastic and the result was just about the perfect surface. Plastic is necessary because my Thick Paintings will stick to almost anything else; but some padding also seemed desirable because the freshly applied paint remains a little soft for some time, and all will become a little pliable in really hot weather. The padding would cushion the work against the pressure of its own weight and hence retard the flattening of supporting surfaces, but it was incapable of giving the firm support that *Beer Bottle* needed in the upside-down position, so I would rest it on the particle-board floor that had been laid in that section of the basement. The most conspicuous effect of flattening that resulted

was welcome in this instance, since I wanted to create a more stable upper surface.

If the pressure on the base of the piece was less while it rested on the bench in the upright position because the weight was distributed over a larger surface, it was evidently sufficient to hold back the development of such tiny pimples as I had first noticed on *Apple*. Pimples did occur around the sides of *Beer Bottle*, and proceeded to develop, first into ripples and then into quite large undulations. As with *Apple*, the progressive loss of regularity of surface resulted quite naturally and spontaneously in my applying paint more loosely. Conversely, as the weight of the piece resting on the upper and lower surfaces resulted in a smoother form, I found I had to brush out paint more smoothly. Irregular brushing of paint over a regular surface would have been very hard to justify visually. Hence the interplay of sensibility and process tends very conspicuously in *Beer Bottle* to intensify the diversification of vertical and horizontal surfaces, and gives the piece its particular character.

Beer Bottle has been shown three times, in *On -ing and Paint* at Regina in 1980, in *Bent Axis Approach*, and, most recently, as part of my contribution to Ron Shuebrook's *News from Nova Scotia* exhibition at Harbourfront Gallery in Toronto. I have tended to choose it because its compact form makes it easy to pack and unlikely to be damaged by minor jolts. As of July 17th, 1985, it has accumulated 2162 half-coats and measures nine inches in height by seven inches in diameter.

Egg (Plate VIII)
This was certainly one of the very first pieces started, perhaps on the morning after the first afternoon. I believe I painted it from the first with the small No. 6 brush and set the pattern of directing brushstrokes longitudinally along the egg, making them converge towards the centre at each end. The division of half-coats was along the longitudinal axis, but I made it fall along a different line every time. I think I did anticipate, even at that stage, that there would be some bulging where half-coats overlapped and the thickness of the paint was doubled, though I certainly could not have predicted the sort of knife-shaped ridges that many pieces have produced. Even if it was just a matter of bulging, however, I particularly wanted to avoid that possibility with this piece, since it was the regularity of form, as much as the fact of potential life and all of the symbolism that follows from that, that had attracted me to the egg as a base for a Thick Painting. I clearly remember spending a long time brushing out paint until it was so smooth and consistent I might have said "absolutely smooth."

Of course, what I perceived to be absolutely smooth coats of absolutely even thickness still admitted the possibility of irregularities beyond the limits of my perception. But as the character of these irregularities began to become apparent with the accumulation of layers, what I described on *Beer Bottle* as a ripple emerged on *Egg* with much more precisely wave-like forms all round it, spaced at quite regular intervals from one end to the other. Simple attractiveness is not a quality I am very much interested in achieving in my work, but I must admit to having found this effect attractive. I made a slide of the work at that stage, but I overcame any temptation to leave it just the way it was. As I worked, still making brushstrokes run longitudinally along the egg but finding it increasingly difficult to apply smooth coats over an undulating surface, I found myself allowing the paint to become more fluid, just as I had with *Beer Bottle*, and in time, the shape bulged in all sorts of directions, and one had to look much harder for such rhythmical continuities as might underlie the superficial shapelessness of the expanding form.

As the weeks, and then months, passed, and I saw the quite pronounced development of ridges on other Thick Paintings, I convinced myself that though rotating *Egg* on its axis each time I began a new full coat would suppress their formation, the fact that I was constantly overlapping half-coats at each end should cause points to appear there. In fact, the piece did grow more at the ends than elsewhere, but the end projections did not take off in the way the ridges had on other pieces. After a considerable time, I decided to help things along. After painting each half-coat and then replacing the work on the bench, I would lightly touch each end with a fully loaded brush and allow a tiny peak of paint to adhere. This soon caused the work to conform to my earlier anticipations, but I worried about whether this was in some way making it less authentic, so I stopped. After some time I started again, but now only "peaking out" the grey coats. Then I thought about it again and decided that specific interventions like this were not only permissible, but necessary, if my work was not to imply a fatalistic subservience of my human powers of choice. When I finally recommenced, it was a moral decision.

There was always a bit of a problem making *Egg* balance on the bench, and I think it must have lost quite some quantity of paint through the years by rolling it over onto the wet side. As the shape became more irregular, this really only made things more difficult. Fortunately, a remedy was close at hand, because I always stand this piece close to the jars of grey and white gesso from which I work. It was natural enough to use the plastic lid of the jar to prop up the piece if it showed any tendency to topple over. Recently, however, as the points at each end began to achieve a more pronounced extension, I became aware that they were not in line.

It became more important to have the piece resting absolutely level so that I could judge more precisely how to apply those final touches of paint on each point if I wanted to redirect its lateral extension exactly along the central axis. In order to assure the piece was resting absolutely level, I started using four plastic bottle lids as supports, and these all leave the imprint of their serrated edges where the work has rested against them. To speed the restoration of a true axis between the extending points at each end I now also, once again, began applying a final touch of paint to both points after the application of every half-coat. I have now just managed, more or less, to correct the placing of the central axis, and I believe the sense of precision in the identification of that axis between the points also had the effect of allowing the looser forms that the accumulating layers of paint produced elsewhere to reveal more clearly their own more fluid principles of order.

Egg has now, as of July 18th, 1985, accumulated 2600 half-coats of paint and measures almost sixteen inches from point to point and seven inches in diameter. It may be because it would be quite hard to crate (given that the points must be quite fragile) that I have never shown it. After 1045 half-coats, on June 29th, 1981, I changed to a No. 8 brush and still continue to paint it with this size, holding the body of the piece in my left hand and always having the same point coming toward my body, as I apply the brush back and forth along the surface. I am inclined to think this way of working — with the same end always towards me — has brought about a quite subtle differentiation of the two ends of the work.

Cup, Saucer, and Spoon (Plate IX)

Egg and *Cup, Saucer, and Spoon* have in common the fact that from the start both were painted with radially directed brushstrokes; those with which *Egg* is painted, as I have described, converge on each end, while with this piece the brushstrokes on the saucer have always been painted outwards from the centre, both on top and underneath. They are the only pieces that do this, but I cannot be sure they were begun one after the other.

The particular cup, the particular saucer, and the particular spoon were ones I had brought with me to my Scotia Towers apartment in Halifax while my wife and three children were in England. When I gave up a tenured position at the University of Guelph to become Director of the Graduate Program at Nova Scotia College of Art and Design in 1976, I was at first given only a three-year contract. So we decided that until we saw how things would work out, I would come on my own to Halifax. Had they not worked out, I might well have gone back to England. That was why the best of everything we had went with my family, while I brought the minimum

I could manage with and things we really did not care about. The cup and saucer had been bought with Green Shield trading stamps and were definitely not our best china. The cup had a squarish form with vertical sides, slightly gripped-in at the bottom. It was basically white medium-weight stoneware with alternating circular and rectangular black line motifs, each with flowers at the centre. The centres of the rectangular forms on the cup were filled in with a pale lemon yellow, while on the saucer, the circular forms were touched with yellow. My wife thinks the spoon I used was one we bought in a hardware shop at the bottom of the Headrow in Leeds. When I started to paint them, the cup was sitting on the saucer in the normal way and the spoon resting in the saucer, also in the normal way, with its handle roughly parallel with the handle of the cup. I have always thought of it as a tea cup, even though it could have served as easily for coffee. The fact was, I drank tea almost incessantly while I was living on my own in Scotia Towers (far more tea than beer), and I may have had some idea of imputing a connotation of Englishness to this piece. The gesso itself was all I used to stick them together, and after my experience with *Pair of Shoes*, I had no doubts at all that it would prove an effective adhesive.

I used a No. 6 brush and painted very carefully, trying particularly hard to keep the inside of the cup smooth. I drew the brush vertically up the inside and around the outside of the cup and finally drew it out away from the centre in painting the inside of the saucer. There was really very little choice but to allow the junction of half-coats to coincide with the rim of the saucer, but I knew I did not want to allow a ridge to develop outward from there, leaving the cup marooned in the centre of a great ocean of white gesso. So when I turned the piece over and rested it on the rim of the cup to paint the underside of the saucer, I always made a point of pressing the brush very decisively over the edge of the saucer to curl up any ridge that might develop towards the top of the cup. Almost to my surprise, that worked. But in spite of all my efforts, the inside of the cup filled in very quickly. It filled in more quickly at the bottom than at the top, the vertical sides seeming to tilt inwards to make an inverted cone form, but before much longer that filled in too. I remember a stage when the opening at the top had been reduced to about half an inch. The rim round about had grown to perhaps an inch thick and presented a great rounded ring. In retrospect, I see it like some huge tractor tire in miniature, but maybe a doughnut might make a better literal comparison.

The pressure on the top, when it rested on the bench upside down, kept it pretty level all along, and as always happens, my brushwork responded to that level surface by working each new application till it was smooth. Further down, the sides undulated in an irregular way, but the radiating brushwork on the saucer produced a pronounced pattern of brushmarks that developed into three-dimensional forms. Underneath, the centre of the saucer stayed level under the pressure of the piece resting on it, just like the top of the cup, but the sides developed radiating forms just like the upper part of the saucer. I still remembered to press the brush over the edge as I was finishing off each stroke on the underside, so the outer edge slowly built up, and the paint level in the saucer began to rise quite markedly. When the inside of the cup finally filled in, the paint in the saucer must have been about halfway up the side of the cup.

What always happens when a surface becomes very irregular (unless I make a very deliberate effort to do otherwise) is that I find myself applying paint very loosely and hence compounding the development of irregularities. This is what happened with *Beer Bottle* and *Apple*, also with *Egg*, but the situation with *Cup, Saucer, and Spoon* was not quite the same. With those other pieces I would simply put the paint on and leave it; but with this piece, I would put the paint on, more or less any way, and I would then go round the whole 360 degrees twice, pulling the brush outward towards the edge. I treated the under and upper sides the same way, apart from that downward pressure at the end of each stroke on the under side, but the results on the upper side were more complex. What I would surmise is that plunging the brush into the pool of paint in the saucer caused some paint to move upwards above the brush and, as I pulled the lower part away, this was left as a thicker protrusion of paint on the side of the cup. The amount involved in any individual instance was not such as to be perceptible, but before long, rounded peaks of paint, up to half an inch long, were pushing diagonally upwards from the side of the cup; and two of them, in the area where the handle of the spoon stuck out from the edge of the saucer, are still having a considerable impact on the form of the piece.

At the beginning, the handles of cup and spoon reached out into space and gave the assemblage a very open look. Both have now, long since, been swallowed up in the growing mass of paint. The generally circular form bulges out at the point where the handle of the spoon sticks out from the saucer, but it is only a bulge, not anything at all suggestive of the handle of a spoon. As the paint in the saucer has risen almost to the level of the top of the cup — and after two changes in the method of juncture of half-coats — the piece has become a fully rounded form, with a large, smooth area underneath, a somewhat smaller smooth area on top, and rounded sides with deeply incised striations bulging out all round.

At a certain stage, I imagined this might really be the piece that would take on the spherical form I had imagined for all of them at the beginning. As the paint in the saucer climbed towards the rim of the cup, swallowing up the spoon, the handle of the cup and even, finally, the lower parts of those half-inch-long peaks of paint, it became clear this would not happen. At that stage it also became very difficult to paint the underside because the paint I had dragged over the edge had now come too close to the bench, so I shifted the area of overlap of half-coats to the middle of the piece. That caused the upper parts to round over just like the underside; but it became clear, after some time, that it was causing the central area to bulge out more rapidly and would eventually have produced a ridge there. The most recent change in procedure involves starting off with the piece in its all-white state and in the upright position. I then paint the upper surface grey, smoothing out the part that has been in contact with the bench, and then radially brushing out more fluid paint over the edge and about a sixth of the way down. Painting the underside and the remaining five sixths of the sides leaves it in an all-grey condition, upside down. While it is in the inverted position, I apply white to the underside, taking the brush about a sixth over the edge. The final half-coat takes it to the upright position and returns it to an all-white state. Having the grey half-coats overlap near the bottom and the white near the top has countered the tendency for a central bulge I noted earlier. Recently I have also found I need to turn the piece on its axis from time to time, as the radially applied strokes evidently do not have the same effect round all 360 degrees. The side furthest away from me will tend to have all the paint brushed off, while the nearer side develops deep striations of liquid paint. The imbalance had gone quite a long way before I realized what was happening and took steps to correct it.

As the piece stands at the moment, the smooth area on top still has a very slight indentation at the centre, all that remains of the inside cavity of the cup. The outer edge of this smooth area is generally circular but at one point it pushes outwards about a quarter of an inch; this is all that remains to show for the handle of the cup. The major appendage to the circular smooth top is the largest of those rounded, upward-pushing peaks of paint, which has now pushed up so far that it too has come to rest on the bench when the piece is upside down. I paint it as part of the smooth area, but it has not yet quite merged with the basic circle. When it does, the circle will probably yield its own identity to the larger, more complex embracing shape.

Cup, Saucer, and Spoon has been shown twice, along with *Telephone Directory* and *Lettuce*, in the *(to be continued)* shows at A Space in 1982 and 1985. People who have seen it there or in my studio have often commented on its sensuousness, and I can see what they mean. That is not to say I can explain why this piece should be more sensuous than the others. As far as I am aware, this is just a by-product of the method of working on the piece. Even though I was once virtually addicted to tea, I have never thought of it as providing a particularly sensuous experience. There could of course be elements in the form that have sparked my sensuality, but I have to admit to not being aware of those either. If people find the piece has a sensuous appeal, and that allows them access to the work, I am pleased about it, though I would hope their response would not stop at that level.

As of July 22nd, 1985, *Cup, Saucer, and Spoon* has accumulated 1988 half-coats and measures just under six inches high. Its diameter is approximately ten inches, but extends out an inch further around the spoon handle.

Crouching Lobster (Plate X)

In a way, the lobsters were a second best, a compromise with practicalities when I thought it might be impossible to paint a fish-shaped fish. The reason I wanted to do that was so I could call it $\iota\chi\theta\acute{\upsilon}s$; and the reason I wanted to call it that was because the use of the Greek word for fish provided the initial letters, in Greek, of "Jesus Christ, the Son of God, Saviour." I hoped to indicate through the use of this title that higher levels of significance should be sought in my work than the identity of the core object (or subject) within the domestic context from which I had taken it. That domestic context is important to me, and I want it to be part of the meaning of my work, along with the string of associations that necessarily attach to each particular object. If the whole adds up to a sort of still-life group, I want that too. I am aware how much of the achievement of modern art has come about within the genre of still-life and I feel very positively about being associated with the tradition of the modern. But the final verdict on the meaning of "modern" is not yet in, and I also want to make it as clear as possible that it is the aspect of Modern Art that probes the structure of reality with which I wish to be associated; the aspect, therefore, that seeks to draw from the special resources of art and the personal resources of the artist some intimation of the containing framework of existence, such as might, in former times, have been provided for art by religion. Primarily, it is through contact with the forces I encounter in the process of painting that I may hope to fulfil this mystical quest, but I also want to engage other kinds of connections that will offer multiple qualifications of this central core of meaning, and partic-ularly in this instance, I want to provide links between my work and the older tradition of art in the service of religion, when the more elevated objectives of art were less open to challenge. I do not want to make religious art; I do not have religious faith, and any mystical insights that would be meaningful for me must apply to the material world; but I do wish to indicate that a desire to "know" the material world is an objective as elevated as the religious quest for enlightenment in the past.

I thought of the concealed symbolism that Panofsky had discovered in the still-life accessories of Early Netherlandish Painting and I wanted to associate my work with that, even though for me the higher level of significance is not something beyond the immediate reality to which the object points as symbol only, but another aspect of the thing itself. I do not recall the use of fish symbolism in the art of fifteenth-century Flanders, but if that divides the reference between the fifteenth century and the Early Christian era, so much the better, because I want all those connections — with art historical scholarship as well as the substance of art history, with the Ancient Greek associations of the Greek word as well as its Medieval Christian context. It is through embedding my work in tradition in this way that I hope to persuade people simultaneously to look to it for such higher meanings and to enhance those meanings by connection and association, as they emerge.

All this, however, seemed doomed when my first attempt to paint a mackerel failed and the piece had to be consigned to the garbage. Hope revived in the form of compromise when I stopped in at Scotia Square to get something for supper on my way home from the College late one afternoon. They were offering tiny oblong packets of lobsters, two to a packet, and so small I could hardly believe there would be enough to eat on them to make it worthwhile. My recollection is they cost only a couple of dollars, but it was the small size as much as the low price that appealed to me. A larger lobster might have been expected to become too heavy under the weight of paint and would offer little possibility that the development of forms in paint would transcend the original shape of the lobster. A shellfish, I told myself, was as much a fish as any other sort of fish, so the use of the Greek word for fish would be no less appropriate. I had little doubt it would be possible to apply paint to the shell without any difficulty. The fact that the lobsters were, of course, already cooked seemed also to guarantee a certain stability until the casing of paint became sufficiently strong to provide its own support. What would be sacrificed in not using a "fish-shaped" fish was the visual aspect of the Early Christian symbol, the sign of the fish. Also, the fact that the lobsters were cooked made them unequivocally food, and to that extent more remote from the creature that had once lived. There was something that made me feel uneasy about using a life to make art, even though that life had already been taken, regardless of my interest in its art application. I am not a vegetarian, but taking an animal life to sustain human life is a very different matter from taking life to make art. Nonetheless, I knew I wanted the connotation of "creature that had once lived" to attach to $i\chi\theta\acute{v}s$, even if that meant also attaching the sense of guilt and enduring the tension between that guilt and the aspiration to an elevated symbolic level that had required the use of the fish. These feelings still attach to $i\chi\theta\acute{v}s$ itself, but as I say, I have never felt that tension with the lobsters. But then, I never really felt they were a satisfactory embodiment of $i\chi\theta\acute{v}s$ anyway.

I had intended to paint only one of the lobsters, but then I painted both. I thought at first I would keep them as a pair, and when a second mackerel became the definitive $i\chi\theta\acute{v}s$, I thought of calling them *Two Small Lobsters*, but eventually they became separate works. It was undoubtedly the fact that their positions made them so different in shape that prompted me to start work on both of them. One was quite symmetrical, with large claws spread out on either side just like the specimen on display in Fishermen's Market on the Halifax waterfront. The other was curled up with just a single feeler reaching forward out of the head to break a very compact outline. The descriptions "crouching" and "extended" presented themselves very casually when I needed terms to differentiate them in my record of half-coats. The first entry to mention either of them specifically is from "27 May" and it reads: "not crouching lobster." I recall I had by that time decided to exploit the fact that the two lobsters presented shapes of very different size because of their positions, even though they were probably about the same weight. The entry for May 27th and the paired dots underneath it for the rest of that page indicate that I had decided to leave it in the state it had reached by that time, while continuing to paint *Extended Lobster*. The first systematic tabulation from September 1979 gives *Crouching Lobster* a total of ten half-coats, which I suspect was an arbitrary figure, since I cannot find any clear indication of previous work. Meanwhile the total given for *Extended Lobster* was 146, and this latter figure had risen to 187 when I evidently revised my estimate of work previously done on *Crouching Lobster* (there are no check marks to indicate any work in September) and gave a figure of fifty for it, with ten in parentheses beside it. It was at this time (that is, the end of October and the beginning of November) that I took the first slides of the Thick Paintings. Several slides show the two small lobsters together.

Crouching Lobster had been painted all over in "lobster colour" while *Extended Lobster* remained white. For a considerable time, I kept open the possibility of painting my Thick Paintings in colours other than white for display, and I would occasionally try out colours just to see how they would look. I remember once painting everything bright red. There are still specks of this red on my work bench that were derived from that experiment. At another time I painted *Lettuce* and several other pieces in a lettuce-like shade of green; and I remember experimenting with several shades of greenish-bluish grey to try and give the mackerel-based $\imath\chi\theta\acute{v}s$ a sense of the fish at its core. It was always just a single colour mixture applied all over and it just got listed with the other half-coats. I eventually dropped this notion because the acrylic paint seemed to produce a coarser finish, obscuring some of the detail that had previously built up; and it lacked the positive quality of white over grey, with the considerable indications that gives of the structure of the final coat of paint.

Crouching Lobster was, in any case, red at the stage I had stopped painting it prior to that entry of May 27th (whether after ten or fifty half-coats), and it remained just as it was then till January 24th, 1980, by which time *Extended Lobster* had accumulated a recorded total of 337 half-coats. For a few days I painted both together. Then, on March 9th, when the recorded total for *Extended Lobster* was thirty-four and for *Crouching Lobster*, eighty-six, I reversed my earlier decision and started painting only *Crouching Lobster*, leaving *Extended Lobster* untouched until July 25th. I added twenty-eight coats over the summer and then withheld paint from it till March 20th, 1981, by which time *Crouching Lobster* was registering a total of 920.

The reason for reversing my initial decision as to which piece to leave unpainted was twofold. On reconsideration, it seemed too obvious to leave the smaller piece unpainted beyond the initial stages; also, dishonest to allow the apparent growth of *Extended Lobster* to be gauged by their relative size, when *Extended Lobster* had actually started off bigger in terms of volume encased, if not in terms of solid mass. The second reason was that the complex forms of claws and feelers resulted in the most extraordinary patterns of growth — of complex ridges, films, and bulges of paint. In front of the head and large claws particularly, the ridges twisted and writhed in all directions until one form would overtake another, merge with it, and yield its own direction to that of the dominant shape. If ever I was tempted to record the development of forms coat by coat, it was with this piece; but, in fact, I took no photograph at all during this period. Rationalizing after the event, I might say that there never seemed a stage at which the form the piece had reached was equal in interest to the process of growth by which it had gotten there, and it was always just too late to start recording that. Even with more foresight, I might still not have made a series of photographs.

I was very much aware of the importance of time in my Thick Paintings, but I was also aware of the difference between the sort of time that can be engendered (by whatever means) in a static visual object and the sort of time that exists in music, literature, or videotape. Perhaps the most abiding lesson of my video works of the mid-seventies was an understanding that mine was a spatial sensibility, not a temporal one: the traces of time must be converted into the spatial terms of painting and sculpture. When I actually did stop painting *Extended Lobster*, I may have felt that the traces of its most intricate growth were already becoming submerged beneath the general accumulation of bulk.

When I recommenced painting *Extended Lobster* on March 21st, I may have done so because the form had lost much of its interest for me in the intervening months. I suspect the reason for that was my inability to envisage the piece as still growing after such a long delay. The sense I have of my Thick Paintings is not just of their past as revealed in the traces of earlier growth beneath the surface, but also of their future. Looking back at slides I have taken and recalling the way they had looked to me at the time, I often think my perceptions are more influenced by anticipations of future change than by the present state of the object at which my gaze is directed. I would hope other people would also get something of that feeling, of a work with a potential future as well as an actual past and present, and I am aware that this must depend on the steadfastness of my commitment to sustain their development until some external factor removes that possibility. Somehow leaving a single piece, *Shoe*, without additional coats of paint for several years still looking like a shoe encased in paint does not seem to detract; but deciding to stop another piece because it "looked good" might leave open the possibility of eventually stopping every piece because I was afraid of spoiling it. I would not wish to admit to attaching that much importance to visual attractiveness or to burden the piece with the weight of that admission. *Shoe* had hardly begun to develop at all so it does not carry the same suggestion that I am just working on each piece until some quirk of form should catch my fancy. One final consideration was that had I stopped work on *Extended Lobster*, it would have become, to that extent, just the same as *Shoe*, and I wanted each piece to be different.

The final major change in my working routine with the two small lobsters came about not very long afterwards, when I started painting *Crouching Lobster* with a No. 12 brush. At first I had used a No. 6 on both and had applied paint with extreme care, respecting every intricacy of detail of feelers and small claws. As time passed and paint accumulated, however, it was inevitable that those details would be submerged. *Crouching Lobster* was actually the second piece to be transferred from the No. 6 group to the No. 12 group. One consideration was that the more rapid rate of growth that might be expected with the larger brush would cause this piece to outgrow the other lobster, even while both continued to accumulate half-coats at an equal rate. This suggests the pieces were still very much paired in my thoughts. Perhaps they necessarily always will be; nonetheless, I think, by this time, I had made a final decision to consider them separate works.

The spread-out form of *Extended Lobster* seemed to leave no option but to paint the top and then the bottom, allowing the joining of half-coats to produce a ridge all round which must, eventually, supercede all the internal intricacies of form produced in the early stages, merging everything into a single, slim, undulating form. The same could have happened with *Crouching Lobster*, because the easiest place to have the half-coats meet would have been around the edge. In the early stages that was exactly what I did, but by the time I switched to a No. 12 brush, I had decided to differentiate it from *Extended Lobster* in this respect also. The problem is, of course, what to do with the piece when wet if the join comes anywhere else. My answer was to rest it diagonally against a half-brick. My objective at first was simply to prevent the development of an encircling ridge, not to have a ridge develop in a different place or different way. Over most of the piece there was sufficient room to keep shifting the line of juncture up and down; but, in front, the vertically curling form of a feeler had filled in to produce a disk-like form, and placing the division of half-coats as I had meant painting one side of it with the first half-coat and the other with the second. That, of course, meant that the ridge round it continued to grow, presenting a slim form at right angles to the general mass of the piece. Eventually it grew until it would press against the surface of the bench when I rested it against the half-brick to dry. I must have positioned it so that the body of the lobster was actually leaning against the brick, while this still-extending disk stuck out in front. As it continued to grow still further and was not able to push its way through the bench, it turned and expanded horizontally over the plastic-covered surface, until there came a time when this flipper-like form at the top and bottom had extended so far (and the original disk had, meanwhile, grown so sturdy) that it would support the weight of the whole piece while it dried, and so I had no further need of the brick.

I have noted several times previously that the rate of growth of ridges is very much faster than the accumulation of paint elsewhere. Consequently, the disk on *Crouching Lobster* soon became as big as the rest of the piece. It extended out in front as well as above and below and then more slowly extended back round the main body of the piece. Meanwhile the weight also increased, and it first became too heavy to hold in my hand while painting and then too heavy to lift with ease. When I would turn it over to paint the other side, I found myself rocking it back onto the more bulbous rear, then swivelling it round and lowering it gently back onto the plastic. Doing this has undoubtedly restrained any tendency to ridge at the rear, but elsewhere the ridges have grown very large, leaving the central core containing the lobster as a bulging diagonal block connecting the two horizontal planes of upper and lower flippers. The piece rests on each alternately, as paint is applied to one side and then the other.

A problem arose as the size of the flippers increased. This piece had shaped itself in such a way that a section across it would take the form of the letter Z. This Z-shaped section was slowly distorted by the extension of upper and lower horizontal forms, and pressure from their weight tended to crush the body of the piece very slightly and seemed as if it might cause it to topple over. I countered this imbalance by fixing under one side little drops of paint that had fallen onto the bench and dried. I would fix these disks of paint in three places, where they gradually built up to form props that would stabilize the piece again. Even though both sides of the piece were showing the same signs of distortion due to weight, I applied these disks of paint only to one side, which then definitively became the base. I would add these disks to the three appropriate places on the base, fixing them with a little dab of wet paint when the base was due to be painted, and I would then immediately proceed to paint the whole of the base side, taking care not to dislodge the disks as I did so. Once the paint dried, the disks would become very solidly secured to the surface. I began attaching these drops/disks of paint some time ago and have intermittently resorted to this expedient whenever the piece showed signs of overbalancing. As the most recently applied disks always seem to resemble nipples, the round forms that develop around them with the accumulation of subsequent layers of paint take on a remarkably breast-like character.

Crouching Lobster has accrued a total of 2621 half-coats according to my records. It is six inches high and measures just over twenty inches in length and about eighteen inches across. It has never been exhibited.

Extended Lobster (Plate XI)

Little needs to be added to what has already been noted by way of comparison with *Crouching Lobster*. Once the intricacies of form around feelers and front claws were submerged within the general mass, it became a remarkably simple piece, which is not to say it has been without incident. The overall form is now roughly circular with a single ridge extending continuously all the way round at an approximately constant distance from the bulging forms at the centre, which still indicate fairly clearly the position of the lobster. The surrounding ridge does not quite go straight out to the side but dips gently downwards for about three quarters of the way round. The remaining section in the region of the tail dips more steeply downwards at the right and actually lifts up at the left. There have been times when the edge of the ridge has come to rest against the bench while it is drying, and on several occasions this caused the heavier accumulation of paint that gathers there to spread out against the plastic, producing an irregular extension breaking away from and altering the character of the contour in that area. When I turn the piece over, its shallow cone-like form necessitates allowing it to tip over to one side; this produces a situation that has frequently led to the sudden appearance of such irregularities. For some time now, I have prevented this from happening by running my finger along the parts of the edge where it is liable to happen, after completing each half-coat. A further feature, which has developed quite conspicuously in recent months, is the emergence of a series of undulations in the upper surface in an area about two inches square to the rear and left of the tail, the same area where the contour rises up rather than dipping down.

The direction of brushstrokes when I began most pieces was not very consistent, nor was I usually very conscious of their alignment. Sometimes that will continue to be the case, but with some other pieces a very precise orientation suggests itself and demands to be adhered to strictly thereafter. Both lobsters proved to be of this type and, even though their forms are now so very different, both are alike in that they have tended towards brush movements running longitudinally over the piece, and both further suggesting the bending of brushstrokes round the central bulk of the form. Now that after 2072 half-coats as of July 24th, 1985, *Extended Lobster* has grown to eighteen inches across, brushing out the paint to a visually even film with brushstrokes running in just the right direction represents quite a challenge with the small No. 6 brush.

My method for both sides is the same. I remove it from the bench where it rests between applications and place it on a crate from one of my exhibitions, which is in a better-lit area of the studio and on which I paint several other pieces too. There was a time I held *Extended Lobster* in my left hand to paint, but for perhaps a year, it has been too heavy for this. Having placed the piece so that the central axis of the lobster — and hence the brushstrokes — are aligned with my body, I apply paint to the area to the left of the central bulge around the body. My brushstrokes at this stage generally follow the appropriate direction, but I apply the paint quite loosely with short strokes. Having covered all of that area, I then begin brushing out the paint with longer strokes that reach about a third of the way along the length of the piece. At this stage, I keep my wrist rigid and swing the brush back and forth from the elbow, trying to set my arm to a natural rhythm that I can sustain until the paint comes just right. Besides orienting the marks of the brush, part of what I seem to be doing here is drying out the paint through the friction of the brush, so that it will produce a heavier, more opaque film than is possible when I first apply it. I begin by brushing out the part of this left section at the rear, which is to say, closest to myself. When that is satisfactory, I move on to the central section, making sure it integrates smoothly with the rear part already painted. When the front third is also complete, I may swing the brush over the whole length of the piece, but I do this very lightly, and I am sure I only touch the surface here and there. Having completed the left section, I move onto the central section and then the right section, treating each in essentially the same way and dividing each into thirds for the final brushing out. As a result of this way of working, the central area of the body tends to produce a rather tighter curve at the left where paint from the left section overlaps the central section. This gives a distinctive type of curvature to the form that I have noticed with other pieces also. As with *Alarm Clock*, I have found that the area at the right is more difficult to keep smooth than the area at the left, and I assume that is because curving the brush round the left of the piece simply requires swinging the forearm from a stationary elbow, whereas curving it in the opposite direction also requires movement from the shoulder. I am rather agreeably surprised, however, that the right side of *Extended Lobster* has shown only a hint of a tendency to break into bumps, bulges, and ripples. In fact, this is, perhaps of all the pieces, the one in which I have been able to make the brushstrokes grip and describe the form most tightly. This may have to do with the fact that I have worked on it in the same way for some considerable time, allowing myself to become thoroughly familiar with its response to the brush, completely programming my arm to its rhythms, and fostering, through the interaction of paint with my arm movements, a system of forms (and minute surface grooves left by the bristles of the brush) that are responsive to my arm movements and my sensibility. This cannot go on for ever, however. Eventually the piece will grow too large and the swing of my arm will be over-extended. Until it actually happens, I am not able to predict how I will adapt to the new situation.

Extended Lobster has been shown only once, in my installation

Tunc Autem Facie ad Faciem ad Faciem, at Optica in January 1982.

ΙΧΘΥΣ (Plate XII)

As I have already indicated, my first attempt to paint a mackerel preceded the two small lobsters, but it ran into difficulties. The problem initially was getting the paint to stick to the surface. I began in the usual way, painting one side, waiting for it to dry, and then turning it over to paint the other side. I remember I worked with it on a dinner plate. Unfortunately, the paint did not adhere at all consistently to the scales of the fish, and this was made worse by the fact that the surface was never quite dry. When I turned it over, it would tend to soften, and pieces would stick to the plate while I was trying to patch up the other side. After a few days it began to decay, and all sorts of unpleasantness would ooze out of it and get mixed up with the paint. I thought of the woman in my painting class at Guelph who had preserved her gesso-coated apple by keeping it in the freezer, but she must have let it thaw out before she painted it. When I tried to apply gesso to the ice-cold fish, the gesso froze to it. It froze on in thick irregular chunks and it could not dry until the water evaporated, and for that to happen it had to melt first. In desperation, I went to the opposite extreme, putting it in the oven. But that caused the already somewhat decayed fish to break up more as it started to cook — and, of course, cooking it made it connote "food" rather than "once-living creature." In the meantime, it was rapidly losing its fish shape and yet still had not established a stable casing of gesso. So I threw it in the garbage.

I have already described how I started painting *Crouching Lobster* and *Extended Lobster* as a substitute for the failed mackerel, and I have also indicated my dissatisfaction with that compromise. At the very end of May, I bought another mackerel from Fishermen's Market and tried again. This time, I made a compromise of a different sort, a compromise in my working method. Instead of turning the fish over after each half-coat, I would lay it out on the plate, apply a half-coat of paint to the exposed side, wait for it to dry, and then paint the same side again. I would do this as many times as possible in the course of that day. My records show I applied six half-coats to the mackerel on May 30th. An "A" beside the entry of half-coats for May 31st and a "B" beside the recorded twelve half-coats for the first day of June show how the work progressed. After allowing the paint applied through the day to dry as much as possible overnight, I would turn it over the next morning and work on the other side the whole of that day. For the first few days the underside would be swimming in blood (and whatever other liquid) that had oozed out of the fish overnight, but the damp layer of gesso retained sufficient firmness that I could gently dry it off with a paper towel and proceed to work on it pretty well straight away.

On June 2nd, I applied eighteen half-coats to side A; on June 3rd, twenty-four half-coats to side B; on June 4th, eighteen to side A; and on June 5th, seventeen half-coats to side B. By now the piece had accumulated 102 half-coats in all, and I was sufficiently confident with the results that my record for the next day shows I then did work on both sides. I remember that as the days went by, the liquid I would find underneath the fish in the morning turned from red to brown; but there was less of it. After a while it became just a blotch around the mouth and at two points on the belly. And then the mouth sealed up, though the belly gave me some anxious moments. It was not simply that the flow of noxious liquid continued for several days longer despite all my efforts; a crack in the skin of gesso began to appear on one side about a quarter of an inch from the base and opened up quite wide. However, the rest was by now well sealed, and I continued to paint, working over the open wound till a skin of paint formed over it and the piece finally became stable. But that incident had its effect on the subsequent form of the work, and the effect is still discernable now. At its maximum the wound in the belly opened up so wide that the lowest quarter of an inch of that side turned right under and could not be painted while the fish was that way up. I did, of course, reach it the next day, when I turned the fish over, but the result was that the ridge that developed at the lower overlap of half-coats did not follow the line of the belly all the way along but moved over towards the side with the wound for about three inches. Nonetheless, it did become stable, and after a while I was able to work on it just like any other piece.

There were some other incidents that stand out in my mind. One was the way, just as the mouth sealed up, a small bulge appeared in that area, as if the fish were blowing a bubble. Evidently it had to do with the emission of gases as the flesh decayed; but it still looked uncanny, even though there could be no doubt at all that the fish was decaying. That was the hottest summer I have encountered in Nova Scotia, with the temperature at that particular time soaring into the mid-nineties. I could only make the heat in my apartment bearable by putting the door on the chain and then wedging a coke can at the bottom to keep it a few inches ajar, which allowed cool air to filter through from the air-conditioned corridor outside. I was afraid the increasingly intense smell might cause the neighbours to complain, but the flow of air was generally from the corridor into the apartment, and nobody complained. At the other end of the apartment, I had the windows open behind screens. The smell seem to have flowed that way and attracted a tiny fly, which managed to force its way through the mesh and then land on the wet paint on the fish and stick to it. I was surprised that it left no trace as I applied subsequent coats of paint. The bubble the fish had blown was quite a conspicuous feature for more than a year afterwards.

When I left for England at the end of June, the fish went to my office in the College, where it sat on my desk, along with all the other pieces on which I was working, until my return at the end of August. I was told it nearly did not survive. At least, people said they had considered disposing of it because of the intensity of the smell. It was, apparently, especially bad when the secretaries arrived in the morning, but once they had opened the windows, things slowly improved through the day. By the time I returned, the weather was getting cooler, so I escaped the worst, but the smell in my basement studio was quite distinct for three years afterwards.

In order to get the fish sealed in, I had had to work very quickly on $i\chi\theta\acute{u}s$ in the weeks before my departure. Its total of 382 half-coats was more than a hundred ahead of any other piece. Through the fall of 1979 I worked on it steadily but — now that the gesso casing seemed very securely stabilized — without any sense of urgency. In the spring of 1980, this was one of a dozen pieces on which I worked at an accelerated pace, while several others were left unpainted. At that time my approach was still not as systematic as it has since become, but I seem to recall the pieces I left unpainted were those which seemed to have reached the most satisfactory state visually. I assume it was for that reason, too, that I suddenly stopped painting $i\chi\theta\acute{u}s$ on May 8th, 1980, when it had 770 half-coats, and I did not resume for just over two years. Hardly had I started again than I decided to switch from the No. 8 brush with which I had painted it up to that time to a No. 12 brush. It was only after that time that the features that now appear as its most distinctive characteristics began to become prominent. This has to do particularly with the formation of ridges, which is quite unlike that of any other piece. The reason for this goes back to the modification I had had to make to my working method so as to get the piece started.

When I start off in the usual way, the area where the second half-coat overlaps the first is painted out smoothly, and until several layers have accumulated, there is no indication of thickening in that area. When it does begin to emerge, it does so smoothly, a gentle undulation at first, building up into a more steeply arched form, which finally breaks into a sharp ridge. When that stage is reached, subsequent applications will go up to the edge of the ridge but not over it. When I started painting the mackerel, applying as many as twenty-four half-coats to one side only, the result was an accumulation of paint of sufficient thickness that its edge could not be smoothed away by the application of eighteen half-coats to the

other side the next day. The form of a mackerel around the belly already comes to a sort of ridge, so the twenty-four layers from one side and the eighteen from the other simply went as far as that line, and everything would have developed in the usual way, had not the belly burst, and even that only had the effect of making the ridge veer to one side. The upper part of the mackerel is more rounded because of heavy muscles to either side of the spine. When I would apply a half-coat to side A, therefore, the brush would not stop exactly at the line of the spine, but would slip over, perhaps as little as a one-quarter inch onto side B. As the same thing continued to happen with subsequent coats, a thin step of paint would have built up at the top of side B by the end of the day. Painting that side the next day would not cause the removal or obliteration of the step but, rather, would create another one through the slipover onto side A. In subsequent days, the thicker the paint became, the more pronounced the step, and the more likely, therefore, the next half-coat would find its same natural limit in the same place. By the time I reverted to my usual method of alternating half-coats from one side to the other, the steps were so well established that they continued to form the upper boundary of half-coats and hence continued to grow. Before too long I became aware of what was happening, but in this instance, I made no attempt to counter the tendency. At length, the steps became ridges, one on either side of the spine as well as the single somewhat erratic one underneath the belly. For some time still, the ridges were somewhat irregular and intermittent projections. As the months went by and the half-coats accumulated, the ridges sharpened out into more blade-like forms and these slowly joined up, not only along the back and belly, but also around the head and tail. It worked out that the ridge on the right side of the back linked up with the ridge over the head, while that to the left linked up with the ridge going round the tail; and that meant that there were no longer three ridges, but only a single blade-like form spiralling round the piece, beginning on the right somewhat behind the middle of the back and going from there forward over the head, along the underside, around the tail, and along the left side till it finally disappeared somewhat to the left of the head. The initial stages of this development were evidently laid down while I was working with the No. 8 brush, but extension of the ridge into space around the mackerel became much more rapid once I started to use the No. 12.

The unique configurations of paint that grew up in the area between the ridges on the spine remain to be considered, as do some lesser details. I need to explain that my way of working was always to have it laid out in front of me with the belly closer to me and the spine further away. When I painted one side, the head would look to my right and the tail would be at my left. When I turned it over, the head would be at my left and the tail at my right; but in each case, the belly was towards me, and I painted the piece with horizontal brushstrokes running from head to tail; and the spine was always away from me. As the ridges on either side of the back grew to an inch or more in width, it was impossible for me to see and difficult to reach the area between them without moving out of position. Rather than interrupt the rhythm of my arm movements, I would simply swing the brush between the ridges, back and forth along the spine. What happened was that the paint did not catch evenly all the way along but broke up into patches in some places, smaller spots in others, and sometimes into areas of tiny specks. Since these patches, spots, and specks were now slightly raised up, the tendency was for the brush to catch the same places when subsequent half-coats were applied. In this way a surface began to form that has no parallel in any other piece. A generally grainy intermixture of grey-and-white speckles gives way here and there to rounded pebble-like shapes, which set off the general graininess with their own irregular rhythm. At times, the configurations have seemed suggestive of coastal formations, the sort of area where sand gives way to pebbles and then rocks. The associations seem appropriate to a fish subject, as did the liquid rippling rhythms that simultaneously emerged on the outside of the ridges surrounding the fish.

For a long time, detailed forms of the fish, including the eye and the final bubble it had blown out of its mouth, remained quite distinct, but when I started using the No. 12 brush they rapidly faded. There may have seemed a danger that the general fish-like form of the fish would also eventually fade, and it may have been this that caused me to adopt a practice that reaffirms the visual identification of the work with the fish. Having brushed out the paint as regularly as possible with generally horizontal strokes, I then take the same large brush and draw the simple outline of a fish over the area containing the actual body of the mackerel. Starting above the tail, I make a single curve with a sweeping movement of the brush, down below the body as far as the front of the jaw. I then make another curve in the opposite direction, over the head and back and then, crossing over the first curve, under the tail. What I am doing is not only drawing the fish, but also making the sign of the fish, as I understand this was the formula in the Early Christian period. I am, therefore, simultaneously enhancing its religious connotations and making a token reference to pictorial tradition of the painting materials I am employing. The sign of the fish has an iconic base; it is a picture of a fish, albeit in a very rudimentary form.

My not-altogether-certain recollection is that I began finishing off each half-coat of $\iota\chi\theta\acute{\nu}s$ with the sign of the fish about the same time I changed to a No. 12 brush in 1982. I should say that my actual practice has been to make the sign twice, retracing the track back from the base of the tail to the mouth to the top of the tail. I did this to make the line clearer, but I have no way of knowing how it might have influenced a quite strange effect that has occurred almost all the way along the line on both sides. A quite pronounced ripple of rather large size has emerged at right angles to the direction of the brushstroke, which means of course that the raised-up strips run vertically across the body of the fish. The response of several people who have seen the piece is to express surprise that the scales of the mackerel should still be visible under so many coats of paint. The texture is not really very much like fish scales, but I am interested that people should be so eager to see resemblances of that sort, much as, in years gone by, people would demand to know of abstract painting: "What's it supposed to be?" The fact is, in any case, that the surface of $\iota\chi\theta\acute{\nu}s$ was quite smooth in the area of the fish's body before I began to make the sign of the fish over it and had been so virtually from the start. Fish scales fit together very closely, presenting a very nearly smooth surface which, I assume, must allow the fish to glide through the water more easily.

A few months ago something went wrong with $\iota\chi\theta\acute{\nu}s$, which caused me, for the first and only time, deliberately to alter the shape of a Thick Painting. Normally shapes just emerge out of the process, and even though I never simply accept what happens uncritically, I try to resist, accommodate, or compromise through modifications or adjustment of the process itself in subsequent applications of paint. Very often I will find I have done this unconsciously before even becoming aware that the piece is not the same any more. Perhaps the trouble this time was that I responded too consciously, and tried to force the process too deliberately to produce a particular shape. What had caused me some unease initially was that the area between the double ridges along the spine seemed to be closing in, producing an extended oval form within the wall of ridges and interrupting the spiral flow of the ridge all the way round the contour of the fish. It seemed to me a solution might be to persuade the ridges to extend further along the body in each direction. There was not much room for the left ridge to extend further towards and beyond the head, so my attention focused mainly on the right ridge, which arose from the smooth surface of paint quite a long way forward of the tail. It seemed to me the smooth paint might be very slowly encroaching, and it did not seem too difficult to contrive subsequent applications so as to reverse the tendency.

On the next application, I used a loaded brush and very carefully laid down a line of paint extending the ridge three inches back towards the tail. I went over the brushstroke a second time, so as to cause the paint deposit to bulge on the upper side where I wanted the ridge to form. I brushed in the rest of that side in the normal way, but thinned out the paint in the area above the new ridge line and left a very thin strip immediately above it bare. It was not hard, through repeated applications, to cause the ridge to build up, but I was always very uncomfortable with the results. It may have been that I had miscalculated that the line along which the kind of brushwork I was using might plausibly have generated a ridge formation, but I think I was even more distressed by the fact that it looked contrived, unauthentic. The area behind the new ridge also looked odd, failing to produce the "pebble beach" effect and leaving the horizontal lines of the edges of an increasing number of paint applications exposed. I also became aware of a feature of this side I had not taken into account, and which, in retrospect, seemed likely to have caused me to regard this as the top of the piece, the part that I always had uppermost when I showed it to visitors in my home. Rather too late, I realized how important it was for the visual unity of the piece that the inner surface of the left ridge and the outer surface of the right ridge should flow together in the way they had. Extending the right ridge back interrupted that flow and destroyed a sense of spatial complexity. The piece reduced itself to two almost flat planes, with a separate pebble-beach gap in between; and it suddenly seemed much more obvious and much less interesting to have made the drawing of a fish on that flat surface.

By the time I became sure I had made a wrong decision, the development of the ridge was too far advanced to be undone by just reverting to the old manner of applying paint. I was also aware that I had committed the piece to Ron Shuebrook's *News from Nova Scotia* exhibition at Harbourfront, and I was afraid of tampering with it now in case it would not be presentable for that show, so I just continued along the same wrong track I had chosen until it came time for the work to go to Harbourfront, where I showed it the other way up.

I was glad of the chance to be away from the piece, because it allowed me to mull over all the options in my mind and be as nearly certain as possible that the course of action I had already decided on before it left was the best one. The day we opened up the crate, I set to work that same evening, sanded down the new ridge and filled in the space beyond it with polyfilla, trying to simulate the sort of form that might have been produced, had I not interrupted my original working method. Next day I sanded down the polyfilla and applied the first grey half-coat. Immediately I felt more comfortable with the piece and have felt increasingly confident with each subsequent application. To my surprise, even though I have

undone the things I did to counter the effect, the area between the ridges no longer seems to be closing in as I had originally feared. All that remains to show for the episode is a half-inch of parallel grey and white striations where the substructure of the new ridge was not completely obliterated by my repairs and a minute glimpse of polyfilla that failed to be covered by subsequent applications of paint. It stands out pink against the more neutral white of the gesso.

$\iota\chi\theta\acute{\upsilon}s$ has now accumulated 1942 half-coats, as of July 26th, 1985. It is twenty-six inches long, fourteen inches wide, and just over five inches deep. It is getting rather heavy and is becoming increasingly difficult to turn over. It has been shown only once, at the Harbourfront exhibition. On that occasion it was displayed under a plexiglas dome.

Ice Tray (Plate XIII)

The ice tray was just a regular plastic one, the sort that goes in the freezer of an ordinary domestic refrigerator. What I cannot remember is whether it was one of the original ones that went with my refrigerator in Scotia Towers or one of an extra set that — I seem to recall — I found in my apartment when I returned from England at the end of the summer, presumably bought by the person who had the apartment while I was away (and who may also have left the book of matches). The ice tray had twelve compartments and a raised rim around the edge to catch any overflow of water. This rim presented continuous straight lines along the sides, and its four corners were smoothly rounded off. I chose to paint it because of the regular repetition of units of space it presented. None of the other objects I had chosen had such a form, and it was important one of them should, so as to make a connection with the grid patterns of my earlier Process Paintings. I also had in mind the modular forms of such artists as Don Judd and Sol LeWitt, for whom I had some regard.

From the beginning, I used a No. 8 brush, even though I anticipated correctly that there would be some difficulty negotiating the comparatively small forms of the compartments. Perhaps that helped them to fill in more quickly than they might otherwise have done, but my experience with the hollow forms of other pieces, such as *Cup, Saucer, and Spoon,* leave no doubt it would have been fairly rapid anyway. Also, from the beginning, I realized there was only one area in which the overlap of half-coats could come — along the sides of the tray; but within the limited space available to me there, I have tried to shift the line of overlap as much as possible. It naturally becomes easier to avoid the formation of ridges along the sides as the piece becomes deeper.

The way the form has progressed is strange in at least one

respect. The spaces inside the compartments have long since filled in, as have the spaces between compartments on the other side. However, the bulging accumulations of paint along the sides (where the plastic rim was straight) still bear a distinct articulation into six parts, and this allows me to confirm that there were, indeed, six compartments on each side, twelve in all.

The task of painting *Ice Tray* became much easier as the compartments filled in, allowing me to swing the brush back and forth along the full length of the piece. There was a time when it seemed very difficult to make the brushwork at each end integrate with the rest, and I am really not quite sure why that should no longer be a problem. On top, the piece now reveals an enlarged, smoothly rounded rim and, inside that, a surface displaying two shallow channels down each side, about where the centres of the compartments must have been. The channels become just a little deeper over the centres of the end compartments. The ripple effect, which I have noted on several other pieces, has for some time begun to affect the centremost part of the interior, further obscuring the original articulation of parts. For a long time, people used to say it looked like an egg box, but I think that resemblance is now disappearing.

For perhaps five years, I held this piece in my left hand while painting it, but maybe a year ago it became too heavy to do this comfortably. Since then I have painted it on the bench, and this seems to have brought about some modification of the pattern of growth, most noticeably that small protrusions of paint have started to grow straight out from several places at each end. Formerly, I used to turn the piece from time to time, so that the same end was not always closest to me while I worked on it. I have now stopped doing that and always have the same end (whichever side is being painted) projecting diagonally over the edge of the bench on my right side. My impression is that that end is beginning to become more bulbous.

Ice Tray has been exhibited only once thus far, in *Tunc Autem Facie ad Faciem ad Faciem*, three and a half years ago. As of July 26th, 1985, it has 2223 half-coats, and measures sixteen by eight and one-half by five inches.

Empty Box (Plate XIV)

If the choice of the ice tray was made with half an eye to Judd and LeWitt, I was no less conscious of the precedent set by Andy Warhol when I decided to paint a box that had contained pan cleaners. Mine, however, was not a Brillo box (Brillo pads were too expensive), but the cheaper S.O.S. It was quite empty when I started, apart, perhaps, from a few strands of metal fibre that still clung to the cardboard deep down inside. I began painting it just the way it was, with the four flaps at the top still open and rapidly fixed in place by the accumulation of gesso around them. To be more precise, three of the flaps were fixed in place open, propped up against each other. The fourth one, a short flap at one end, tipped inside; and as the paint layer grew thicker, the unsupported ends of the longer flaps pulled inwards quite distinctly at that end. I painted just over the edge of the flaps, but made no attempt to reach deeper inside. At first, the opening at the top seemed huge, but my experience with *Alarm Clock* and several other pieces alerted me to be prepared that it would fill in before many months had elapsed. Just before it did, I decided to put something inside it so that I would be able to testify from the sound when I shook it that there really was space inside the piece. It was already becoming so heavy that you might otherwise easily have thought it was solid. What I did actually put inside it was a three-quarter-inch triangle of wood sawn off the end of a house painting brush (I recall the handle was painted green) and almost as an afterthought, through the tiniest chink that remained till the end, a two-inch nail. I added this because I was afraid the wood, being rather light, might stick to the exposed surface of paint inside the upper section; I thought the metal nail was less likely to do so. As of a few minutes ago, I could still hear both objects rattling round distinctly, though shaking the piece at its present weight is something I will not be tempted to do very often.

Empty Box has always been painted with a No. 8 brush and always so that the division of half-coats would come vertically down the middle of the larger sides. This meant laying it on one of the narrower sides. But when I showed it in my installation *On -ing and Paint* in October 1980, I displayed it in the upright position, supported on three nails on the end wall of the gallery, over which slides (including images of the piece itself) were projected. It was then still quite smooth under its 191 half-coats of paint, and it would have been quite easy to prevent ridges forming indefinitely, since the sides of the box provided ample space for shifting the area of overlap of half-coats. Nevertheless, I must have decided I wanted a double ridge to develop exactly down the centre. I have already explained what I mean by this term: sustaining a precise overlap and allowing a sharp edge to form at either side of the narrow platform that slowly builds up. In this case, the band is about half-an-inch wide and has come to extend down each side and under the base. At the top, the open flaps necessarily caused it to be redirected as a single ridge, taking off from the central ridges along the sides and running along the edges of the flaps round the end of the opening, where the three open flaps had propped each other up. As I had continued to apply paint, the line of the ridge acquired a more curvilinear form, coming to resemble a sort of hood. It may have been this resemblance that determined the piece had to be shown resting on its narrow side, so as to bring the hood the right way up. This was how the piece was shown recently at the *News from Nova Scotia* exhibition, the only other occasion on which it has been exhibited.

The development of the double ridge along the sides of *Empty Box* has been one of some complexity. The curvilinear forms of the hood seemed to work their way back along the body of the box and seemed likely, at one stage, to result in very extravagant formations. I have to admit to being somewhat indecisive in my response, first trying to make the paint conform to a more moderate outline, then becoming afraid the result might look stilted or contrived, and finally allowing the ridges to find their natural boundaries again. As I examine the piece now, I can point to forms that result from each of these changes of approach, but I do not feel at all dissatisfied with the visual outcome, which, in the last analysis, is always the crucial factor. Through all my own indecisiveness, the process seems to have managed "to justify the inevitability of its particular forms."

In contrast to the curvilinear shapes around the sides and top, the part of the double ridge under the base has remained straight, regular in width, and even quite soft in outline. This is undoubtedly because as the piece has become heavier, I have always rested it on the lower ridge while painting it. At first I held the work in my left hand. Resting it on the base ridge is a sort of a compromise, because I have never felt I would be able to achieve the arm movements to swing the brush along the full length of the box with the piece resting horizontally on the bench. I am increasingly conscious that eventually I may have to try.

As of July 26th, 1985, *Empty Box* measures fifteen and a half by eight by eight and a half inches. It has accrued a total of 1981 half-coats.

Paper Bag (Plate XV)

I often tell people that this is my one "political" work. That may be the one piece of irony that I have allowed to enter my work. The irony, however, goes no further than the anecdote. I would have painted a paper bag in any case, even if circumstances had not, quite unexpectedly, presented me with a bag that carried political connotations. From my school days, even before I went to university, I had toyed with the notion of producing a still life of brown paper bags. What attracted me was partly the way the brown paper would break into facets, each reflecting light in a slightly different way and offering endless modulations of this basic greyish brown, but I was also fascinated by the way the bags would assume the attitude of landscape and of human posture. I recall that I did actually make the attempt on a couple of occasions, but I never came close to creating an image that seemed in any way satisfactory. The ghost of the idea lingered, however, and I had already decided on building a Thick Painting round a paper bag when the one in question suddenly popped through the letter box. It was the time of a federal election, and Alexa McDonough was running for the NDP. The bag had a card inside it with — if my memory serves me right — red printing on it. It read: "The Liberals and the Conservatives think they have it in the bag, but they had better watch out for Alexa McDonough." In fact, I threw the card away and only painted the bag — a tall, thin, brown paper bag — that would have opened out to a box-like rectilinear form, but which I allowed to close up, leaving only a small wedge-shaped hollow section between the flat base and the upper parts, where the paper sides rested loosely but closely together.

As with *Empty Box*, I used a No. 8 brush and made the overlap of half-coats divide the bag vertically, though I was careful from the start not to allow any sort of ridge to develop. This proved easy enough, since there was ample room to move the area of overlap around. Dividing it that way meant I had to leave it resting on one edge to dry, and that too was easy enough, since the triangular shape immediately above the base and the long line of the upper part of the bag made a quite stable support. I had decided, nonetheless, that I wanted to show the piece standing up, just the way the paper bags would have been in that still life I never managed to paint. This presented a problem because the gesso dried to a rather heavy, leathery skin, quite different in character from the crisp, light membrane of the original paper. Whenever I would try standing it upright, the weight would cause the upper part to sag and plop over limply. I kept hoping the application of more coats of paint would make it stiffer, and I even persevered into the fall after my return from England. But it became clear before many more weeks passed that something had to be done. I slit through the top at the centre, making a tiny opening into the bag itself, and I inserted the slim wooden handle of an old No. 6 brush, sawn off to make it exactly the right length. There was no trouble wedging it in place, or in persuading the top of the bag to seal up again, or, thereafter, in maintaining the upper part in an upright position, not rigidly vertical, but tilting over quite naturally to one side. Of course, the brush handle made a slight bulge in that area, but I could easily compensate for this by using the overlapping of half-coats to build up other parts around it.

There was something I enjoyed about this expedient, almost as much as the circumstances that had provided me with the bag in the first place. I have to admit to being as sceptical about Freudian psychoanalysis as I am about political art, but I could hardly help noting the Freudian symbolism. I wondered if it was a deliberate strategy, The question is largely academic, since no one knowing Halifax could possibly doubt the Liberals or Conservatives would, indeed, have had it in the bag all along.

Paper Bag has been shown only once, in the *(to be continued)* installation at Eye Level Gallery in January 1983. At that time the upper section had grown to perhaps half an inch thick, and there was the very slightest suggestion of changing angle across its width, which was emphasized by the vertical texture of the brushstrokes. Since then, the upper section has more than doubled in thickness, and the lower triangular base has become much more bulky. The only problem I have encountered since inserting the brush handle was that of keeping the base stable. My approach to this has been to use the area of overlap of half-coats to isolate four points of support close to the four corners and to keep them in a single plane. Mainly because of this, it has also been necessary to make the line of overlap take a meandering route across the triangular base before reaching whichever part of the upper section I am locating it on at that particular time (I have always made the overlap run in the same straight line up each side of the upper section). The rippling texture along the line of overlap provides a counterpoint to the lines of the edges, which are kept pretty straight by the piece's own weight as it rests on the bench.

Paper Bag is now rather too heavy to hold comfortably in the hand, but as with *Empty Box*, I have never felt it could be painted standing on the bench. My solution in this case is to allow various parts of it to rest on the bench while I tilt it with my hand to bring it into an appropriate position. In my normal working schedule, *Paper Bag* is painted immediately after *Empty Box*, which itself immediately follows *Ice Tray*. In my own mind, these pieces have always tended to group together.

Paper Bag, as of July 27th, 1985, has 2082 half-coats and stands fifteen inches high. The base measures eight by seven inches.

Newspaper (Plate XVI)

This may have been one of the earliest pieces started; I just do not remember. It early became associated in my mind with *Telephone Directory*, but this may have been because both had a somewhat similar shape and both have always been painted with a No. 12 brush. Only three pieces begun before I left for England at the end of June 1979 were painted with a No. 12 brush, *Pair of Shoes* being the third. The problem is partly that even after I started to keep records on May 8th, I did not do it very systematically. From May 27th to June 10th I have a set of checkmarks which refer to the application of half-coats to several pieces. I noted exceptions like "not crouching lobster" on May 27th, but I did not record which pieces were included. And when I came to total these figures on an undated yellow sheet, which I think belongs to the time immediately before my departure, I simply wrote: "All except crouching lobster and mackerel." The total came to fifty-two, and there then follow computations of additional half-coats applied to some particular pieces. *Newspaper* is not mentioned specifically. When I produced the first fully systematic tabulations on September 22th, *Cup, Saucer, and Spoon, Danish Pastry, Shoe, Ice Tray, Empty Box, Newspaper,* and *Telephone Directory* are all shown as having fifty-two half-coats of paint. I have already indicated my suspicions regarding the possibility that the attribution of fifty-two half-coats to *Shoe* was arbitrary. However, I am inclined to think those particular early checkmarks do apply to *Newspaper*, and I have very little doubt that it was underway by May 27th. What is more seriously in doubt is whether it was being painted before that date. Except in the case of *Crouching Lobster* and *Shoe*, what I seem to have done is simply ignore any painting that was done before May 27th, and just include in subsequent totals half-coats documented by checkmarks. What it means is that many pieces had early accumulated a number of half-coats that are not recorded, though whether that number is ten or fifty is a question I was, even in the fall of 1979, unable to resolve on the basis of my recollection. As regards *Newspaper*, my memory is now a blank on that particular point.

The newspaper concerned was either the Halifax *Mail Star* or *Chronicle Herald*; I am uncertain on that point also. But I am very clear as to why I chose to paint it. The body of paintings I had produced most recently before starting work on the Thick Paintings was my Newspaper Paintings. In retrospect, these might appear as a preliminary development leading up to the Thick Paintings. The earliest ones involved my gluing a piece of newspaper to a masonite panel, simply so I would have a visual given to work to. Subsequently, I would glue all the pages of a newspaper together (or one section of a newspaper). I then worked on this base in various ways. Some were painted with stripes, others with very fine threads of paint laid as close to each other as possible, while still others were left just as they were and depended on the connotations of the red-hot story on the newsstand when introduced into the context of High Art. Finally there were those in which the whole (or, more precisely, all the visible parts) was encased in paint of a uniform colour. This was getting very close to the Thick Paintings, and when I decided to include a newspaper as the base for an actual Thick Painting, I do recall very clearly that I wanted to establish links with the earlier work. This might suggest that the piece itself was early among the Thick Paintings, but, in fact, such deliberately calculated decisions really belong more properly to a somewhat later stage when I had more time to consider the implications of the project on which I had embarked.

One thing that all of the Newspaper Paintings had in common was that they were meant to hang on a wall just like regular easel paintings. When I first began the Thick Painting *Newspaper*, my intention was that it too should hang on a wall, and on the only occasion on which it has thus far been shown, in my installation *Keeping Marlene out of the Picture — and Lawn* at the Anna Leonowens Gallery in Halifax in November 1980, it was shown rather precariously anchored to the wall at eye level with four bent nails. In future, when I show it, it will be presented resting flat on a stand. Given its present weight and the way in which its forms have developed, presenting it in any other way would be out of the question.

Newspaper, like several other pieces (*Cup, Saucer, and Spoon, Pair of Shoes, Alarm Clock, Ice Tray, Empty Box, Paper Bag*, etc.), took as its base an object that had gaps or hollows or concavities in its form, specifically in this case, the spaces between the folds (I folded it down to a quarter of its closed size). As with those other pieces, the most noticeable change in form in the early stages was the filling in of those spaces, which had been complete for some time when I showed it in November 1980. At that time, its form was that of a simple rectangular slab and, to that extent, was somewhat like *Telephone Directory*. The most significant difference, in regard to the future development of form, was that *Telephone Directory* was marginally thicker and had square sides, which made it comparatively easy to shift the line of overlap of half-coats up and down. *Newspaper*, by contrast, had more rounded edges, particularly on the longer sides where the paper was folded over, and this left me with very little choice but to have the line of overlap of half-coats come in the middle of that fold. This, of course, meant a ridge could be expected to develop there. In fact, I was able to influence the development a little, so that the ridge, when it emerged, was not exactly in the middle but closer to the large surface I came to think of as the back or base. I encouraged this tendency until the outside of the ridge became continuous with the plane of that large surface. This meant that when I had painted the other side and laid it down, wet paint along the ridge was likely to come in contact with the plastic on the bench. As I have described elsewhere, this has the effect of producing a much more rapid development of the ridge, but in practice, this happened only along the two short sides and on one of the longer ones. On the three sides where it did happen, however, it was quite rapid, so much so that I became

anxious in case it should become too large to be manageable.

At about the same time, I modified my working method on *Newspaper* in two ways. I decided to halt the extension of the ridge on the three sides where it was prominent by pushing the brush over the edge when I painted the flat side (which I regarded as the underside) in much the way that I had pushed it over the edge of the saucer in order to redirect its ridge. But, in this instance, I continued doing this only until I had lifted the ridge sufficiently to stop wet paint from the other side coming in contact with the plastic. I was able to do this without too much difficulty. The fourth side had hardly developed a ridge at all, and meanwhile the thickness of the slab had grown considerably. By balancing the piece slightly projecting over the edge of the bench when I painted the underside, I was able to carry that half-coat over that ridge and establish a new area of overlap at the other side of the paper. As I have continued to do this, it has not yet initiated a new ridge (though it has produced some marked changes of texture) but seems instead to be building up the area alongside the partially developed ridge, so that there is now virtually no ridge at all along that side. This provides a welcome variation within the formal regularity of the piece, but it has also had an equally welcome practical consequence. Now that the work is getting rather heavy to lift, I anticipate that turning it over will eventually become a problem. Having one edge without a ridge is useful in this regard, because I can now roll it over along that edge. This requires much less effort and is much less awkward than lifting the piece completely. Some other pieces that have ridges all round are now becoming very hard to turn over. This is notably the case with *Pair of Shoes* and $\iota\chi\theta\acute{\nu}s$.

My way of working the large surfaces of *Newspaper* has been somewhat similar to my way of working with *Telephone Directory*, orienting the brushstrokes in alternate coats at right angles to each other. In the case of *Newspaper*, I paint the grey coat across and the white along. The difference is that whereas I have always brushed out the paint on *Telephone Directory* as much as possible, really scrubbing the surface, I have tried to apply the paint much more loosely to *Newspaper*. It may seem consistent that whereas very shallow hollows developed on *Telephone Directory*, an area of quite closely spaced lumps (just a shade smaller than the hollows) appeared quite suddenly on each side of *Newspaper*. It would be wrong, as I found, to infer a too-mechanical relationship between apparent cause and undeniable effect. When these lumps appeared, I decided to try to extend them by working still more loosely. This had no effect, and when I returned to the earlier degree of looseness, this had no effect either. The original series of lumps remained on each side until a few weeks ago, when those on the underside disappeared.

61

The cause of this is less conjectural. It is an irritating coincidence that the summer months, when I have most time to work on my Thick Paintings, are also the time when it is hottest and most humid in my basement studio. The application of more layers of paint compounds the problem of the humid atmosphere and results in the pieces holding more water than in the winter months. A softening of the paint through the presence of moisture is exacerbated by the heat itself (in high temperatures even well-dried-out pieces tend to become somewhat pliable). Moisture naturally tends to accumulate most on the underside, on which the piece rests for longer intervals while I am working on the objects painted with brushes of the other two sizes. The result — I assume fairly confidently — of this combination of conditions is that the area of lumps has recently disappeared almost entirely from the underside of *Newspaper*, the soft paint having been pressed quite flat by the weight of the piece itself.

Newspaper, after the recorded application of 2155 half-coats, has grown to twenty-seven by thirteen inches and is more than four inches deep.

Brushstroke (Plate XVII)

Any account of *Brushstroke* would have to begin with an acknowledgment to Mary Scott, then a graduate student at the College. She had been painting with a hypodermic syringe since her undergraduate days in Calgary. For several months after she came to Nova Scotia College of Art and Design, she worked on a piece in which she used the hypodermic to write out quotations from Gertrude Stein, allowing layer upon layer of them to build up on a plexiglas base. As a by-product of this piece, she produced a much simpler work, in which she wrote out a single line from Stein's writings on a sheet of plastic, then kept on adding more and more lines on top of this until it became perhaps a quarter of an inch thick. The thread of acrylic paint, as it emerged from the hypodermic needle, was fine and regular, but did have some bulk, so that the buildup did not take as long as might have been anticipated, for instance, on the basis of my own layering with the brush. When the piece had achieved a sufficient thickness, she peeled it off the plastic and it was done. She would show it hanging by one end from a nail in the wall.

The fact that paint could be made to stand entirely by itself was the part of Mary's project that was crucial to this particular piece of mine. I took a No. 8 brush, loaded it very fully with Mars Black, and laid down a single brushstroke about three inches long on a sheet of plastic. The square-ended brush produced a brushstroke that was square at each end and of a regular width, maybe just a shade over half an inch. When it was thoroughly dry, I peeled it off the plastic and began applying layers of grey and white gesso to it, just as I would have on any other object. Because I had loaded the brush so heavily, the initial black brushstroke was much bulkier than the layers of paint I normally work with, and there is a difference in consistency between the actual acrylic paint and acrylic gesso that causes the former to retain much more of its bulk when it dries. The single black brushstroke, as it came off the plastic, was still very light, very floppy, and probably quite fragile. It required considerable care at first to apply each half-coat of paint to it, painting one side and then the other, and being especially careful not to let the sort of accumulations of wet paint form along the edge that would spread out on coming in contact with the plastic and distort the development of form. As I persisted, the piece gradually became thicker and firmer. As a ridge began to develop around the edge, the central area became more bulbous, so that it slowly lifted the edges off the bench and substantially reduced the risk of wet paint touching the plastic. The square ends, meanwhile, were rounding out, and the proportions of the shape were changing imperceptibly.

When I began applying layers of gesso to the original black brushstroke made with a No. 8 brush, I used the smaller No. 6 brush to apply the gesso, but I always kept the brushstrokes I made with it parallel with the direction of the original brushstroke. It was the experience of working in this way with this piece that made me realize that paint tends to spread out over the edge of a ridge rather more when the brush runs laterally along it than when it runs straight off across the edge. I would have expected the opposite to be the case, but the evidence of the disproportionately increasing width of *Brushstroke* was incontrovertible; and this continued to be the case when, after two years and 1287 half-coats, I reverted to a No. 8 brush. Now, as of July 28th, 1985, and after 2777 half-coats, according to my records, it measures sixteen and a half inches in length and fifteen inches in width, which is to say it looks almost circular in form, though the length still exceeds the width by one and a half inches. If my recollection of the proportions of the original brushstroke are reliable (three by one-half inches), its length exceeded its width by two and a half inches, which means that the increase in lateral development has exceeded the piece's longitudinal growth by one inch (two and a half to one and a half inches) or 7.5 percent.

That original brushstroke in black acrylic was quite regular in its containing rectangular outline, as I have already indicated, but it had the somewhat irregular internal striations you would expect of any brushstroke made with a quite stiff brush and not subsequently brushed out. My applications of paint to that initial base have been carefully brushed out, and the result has been that initial irregularities have long since disappeared, and the work has taken on a generally regular form, with large convex curves over the central core giving way to slightly concave curves towards the surrounding ridges. As the central area has rounded out, balancing the piece on the bench has occasionally become a problem, and I have had to prop it up with rolled-up pieces of paper. Keeping the plane of the circumference level has been a more serious problem, and I have had to watch it very carefully, running my finger round the edge when any obvious overspill of paint occurred or sometimes just as a matter of routine to correct any tendency in a particular section to veer out of true.

Even though *Brushstroke* has now become quite heavy, I still work with it held in my left hand, cupping my palm under the bulbous central mass and supporting the back of my hand on a firmly positioned left knee as I squat on the floor in front of the bench. The most difficult part is lifting it up on my fingertips afterwards, so that I can see if any paint has spilled over the edge. I still make the brushstrokes run longitudinally along the length of the work and keep them parallel to each other, not allowing them to curve round the central mass (as I do with *Alarm Clock*, which I always paint next after *Brushstroke* and which is stored underneath it on the middle shelf of a three-shelf corner unit next to a cupboard beside my studio bench). I always swing the brush back and forth, away from and towards my body, and try to follow the grooves left by the previous coat. As the piece becomes more nearly circular, it becomes more difficult to maintain the correct alignment, and from time to time, I find myself having to make adjustments. As it gets larger and the curvature of the surface becomes more complex, I find I am not able to swing the arm in a single movement from concave to convex to concave. I have tended, as with some other pieces, to treat it in three sections.

Within the generally smooth contours of the piece, I have experienced some distinctive developments, certain ones influencing the form of the work more permanently than others. The most surprising has been the occurrence of long, extremely narrow bands of rippling form within the striations of the paint. A single band may suddenly appear, or there may be several simultaneously on different parts of the surface. They are less than an eighth of an inch in width and seem to be contained quite precisely within particular striations in the paint. The undulations along their three or four inches also seem remarkably regular, each perhaps rather more than an eighth of an inch in length from the crown of one undulation to that of the next. What I find most surprising is that the bands are so much narrower than the brush, the movements of which must, in some way or another, have generated them. These bands will survive and perhaps develop a little through maybe several dozen applications of paint but then just fade away. At the moment, none are visible on either surface.

As the work has grown larger, a more persistent formation of scale-like protrusions, also little more than an eighth of an inch across, has developed around whichever end of the central bulbous mass is farther away from me as I paint. When I turn the piece round, after a few months, and paint it with the other end away from me, the scale-like protrusions have faded from that end and new, identical ones have again emerged at the far end. Meanwhile, the area within an inch or so of the edge of the ridge closest to me has tended to accumulate a sort of sedimentation. It is not hard to imagine why this should produce forms like the patterns of sand on the beach, the brush leaving a deposit of paint as it slows down towards the end of its swing, much as waves release a deposit of sand as their pace slackens. As the piece gets larger, and it becomes even more difficult for me to extend the swing of the brush, the growth of the deposits becomes more marked. They represent a considerably greater bulk than either of the other effects I have described, and though they tend to merge into fresh accumulations of half-coats when I turn the piece round, it seems quite possible they will result in permanent modifications of the longitudinal section, still further complicating its concave-convex-concave curvature.

Brushstroke has been exhibited only once, in *Bent Axis Approach*, at the Nickle Arts Museum just over a year ago.

Alice's Rose (Plate XVIII)

The title alludes to the episode in *Alice in Wonderland* where the gardeners had planted white roses, though the Queen had ordered red, and were busily painting them red when Alice entered the garden. My decision to paint a rose, however, had much more to do with the fact that a colleague at the College, Kenna Manos, and I share a birthday as well as a connection with Yorkshire. For several years after I began teaching at the College, she would buy me a rose for my birthday and she gave me to understand that the rose had to do with the fact of our connection with Yorkshire. But the rose was always a red rose, which is the emblem of Lancashire, whereas the Yorkshire emblem is a white rose. At first, when I thought she had been born in Yorkshire herself, I was surprised she would give me a Lancashire rose. In fact, it was her father who was born in Yorkshire, and I cannot claim to be a true "tyke" myself, having only worked for ten years at Leeds University. A "tyke" is someone born in Yorkshire, both of whose parents were born in Yorkshire.

The birthday I share with Kenna Manos falls on April 18th, only a couple of weeks or so before I started the Thick Painting project, but by the time I thought of painting a rose, Kenna's rose had wilted and been committed to my wastepaper basket. So I went to the florist's and looked for one as much like the one she had given me as possible. The bloom was only just beginning to open, and it had a long stem with quite a lot of leaves just like Kenna's. When I started, the prospect of painting all that length of stalk seemed ridiculous, so I cut about four inches off the bottom. As I thought about this afterwards, I had an increasingly uneasy feeling that I had compromised the authenticity of the piece by doing this, so a year later when the work was already quite well developed, I cut four inches of privet stem from a hedge by the side of our garden, drilled a hole in the appropriate part of the Thick Painting, and repaired the damage. I was surprised how quickly the paint built up around this snippet of privet stalk and allowed it to merge unobtrusively with the rest of the piece.

Starting to paint the original rose had been very difficult. The paint had been reluctant to stick to the surface of leaves and petals, the shapes were intricate, even for a No. 6 brush, and nothing would keep still. It was hard to find a way of holding it so I could apply the paint, and it was a real problem finding a way of propping it up to dry so that the leaves would remain in their natural position. I remember I tried to balance it in a glass tumbler, but in spite of all my efforts, the leaves rapidly stuck themselves together in a single vertical plane. When this happened there was clearly no point to using the glass anymore, so I allowed it to rest flat on the bench, accepting the contour of the flat plate it now formed as the obvious place for the division of half-coats to occur, and I accepted the implication that a ridge would inevitably grow out from that line.

I was, for some time, rather casual about the way I painted *Alice's Rose*, allowing the brush to find its own way around the forms, without any sense that it might be necessary to establish a particular pattern of brushstrokes. But, after the initial stages, I was consistent in the way I held it while I was painting. I always held it parallel to my body with the bloom on my right, which meant that the stem, and later the piece of privet stalk, were on my left. When I turned it over, the edge that had been closest to my body would be farthest away from me and vice versa, but the bloom remained on my right and the stalk on my left. It follows that when I painted the stalk I had to reach across myself, bringing the brush in contact with the surface at a quite acute angle. When I added the privet stem, I had to reach further, and the angle of the brush became more acute. This undoubtedly explains why I suddenly found I had been missing the very end of the stalk, and by the time I noticed it, there were several rings of grey and white surrounding a central white spot, where alternating coats of paint had built up at the end without ever fully closing over. I noticed the same sort of thing was happening at a point to the left of a bunch of leaves closer to the centre. This took me quite by surprise and was quite at variance with my initial intention to completely surround every object with each coat of paint (or, more properly, with each pair of half-coats). Nonetheless, I decided to allow this development to continue and so kept on painting just as I had been.

The area at the end of the privet stalk expanded very slowly indeed, as I worked. I came to realize that every half-coat did not leave a trace at the edge, but only a small proportion in which the paint would bulge over the edge somewhat further than usual, and then perhaps only in a few particular places. The pattern of squashed rings of grey and white that very slowly pushed its way out towards the side, therefore, gave the impression of considerably fewer layers of paint than I had actually applied. Had it been otherwise, there would have been no pattern of rings at all, since alternating stripes of paint a thousandth of an inch thick would be too fine to discern with the naked eye and would merge into a uniform grey. The rate of growth around the point to the left of the bunch of leaves was even slower than that at the end of the privet stem.

It must have been more than a year before the rings at the end of the stalk began to turn up along the edges of the plate of paint that had formed around the privet stalk and the lower parts of the actual stem. When once they did, they seemed to spread more quickly and, in the course of the next two years or so, they linked up with the other area of rings that had, itself, been expanding at a rather slower rate. As the process continued further, I felt convinced the whole piece would eventually open up, the upper surface on which I applied one half-coat separating from the lower surface on which I would apply the next, as the squashed rings of grey and white eventually extended themselves round the entire length of the peripheral ridge. It was almost like watching a flower bloom. I gave quite a lot of thought to the question of whether I wanted to allow this to happen, but I was persuaded, not only by the unusual effect that the grey-and-white striations along the edge produced, but also by the fact that the normal ridges in other areas were growing very rapidly, and much more increase in size might have made the piece unmanageable. No sooner had I firmly committed myself to this decision, than the process suddenly began to reverse itself, long sections of perhaps an inch or more spontaneously closing in again. This posed quite a dilemma, and I pondered it carefully before deciding, somewhat more than a year ago, to force the issue.

I painted one half-coat in the usual way along the edges that had already opened up, but when I reached the part that was still closed, I painted it very deliberately the smallest distance I could inside the edge, seizing the opportunity to bypass some minor projections in the contour that departed from my sense of the work's overall shape. When I turned it over, I did the same thing with the matching half-coat, and I confined subsequent applications to the new contour this had created. I had been extremely apprehensive that doing this might compromise the integrity of the work, but it seemed only to redirect the natural form-generating properties of the process, not to halt or inhibit them. From the start, the open grey-and-white streaked forms I had deliberately induced merged imperceptibly with those which had come about spontaneously.

When the area at the left around the privet stem opened up, successive applications of paint seemed automatically to overhang the edge in such a way as to produce an even diagonal slope out from the initial spot of white. When I forced the area at the right to open up, the paint seemed for some time not to want to slope out but appeared set on producing a sheer vertical face. I decided that must be the concomitant of the way my right hand caused the brush to come in contact with the right side, but once again, no sooner had I settled into this opinion than the edges suddenly began to slope out very steeply. I decided I did not want that to happen, so again, with some apprehension, I deliberately pulled the half-coats back from the edge. It seems possible to do this without causing an artificial-looking effect because the form the exposed edges of paint layers take on has a highly distinctive character of its own and readily accepts and subsumes such specific modifications as I have, from time to time, forced on it.

The character of these forms is not easy to describe, and I will not attempt to do so. I will point instead to one particular characteristic that seems to play an important part. This has to do with the fact that I always start to paint each half-coat at the left and draw the brush round the edge from left to right before filling in the remainder of the surface. It follows that if there are any irregularities of level along the edge, the brush will press harder against the left side of raised-up sections and will go more lightly over the downward slope to the right, perhaps missing it altogether. As this process is repeated, diagonal wave-like forms grow up in the stratification of grey-and-white paint around the edges. These diagonals always slope back from the central band towards the stem of the plant. To put it another way, they may be conceived as arrow-like configurations pointing towards the flower end of the piece.

If the open edges, which are the most distinctive feature of *Alice's Rose*, have proved remarkably accommodating to all my changes of mind and method, filling in the large surfaces has proved a very exacting task. I have already indicated that I painted these surfaces very freely in the early stages. With other pieces, such as

Apple and *Beer Bottle*, this seemed readily to generate a satisfactory and self-perpetuating character of surface form, but with *Alice's Rose* the results suddenly seemed incoherent and disorganized. It took a great deal of experimentation before I finally settled on a routine that had all brushstrokes running across the form but allowed them to fan out round a central bend in the overall form and then let them curve out round the bulging form at the right, which had built up round the bloom. Even then, I found it necessary to divide up the work into three sections, and the internal areas of join between them have produced rises (rather than ridges), which have recently given me more reason to ponder. My approach at the moment is to allow these rises to develop on one side, which I tend to regard as the underside, but to resist their development on the upper surface by intermittently adopting a four-part division.

One feature of the development of *Alice's Rose* does tend to offset somewhat the difficulties of painting its upper and under surfaces. After the ridge has divided, paint accumulates more quickly along its edges than elsewhere. As the piece progresses, this accentuates the sense of opening up or "blooming." In time I would expect that the peripheral area will become the thickest part of the work, whereas with other pieces the ridge is the narrowest — no more than the thickness of a knife-edge. That extreme development may still be a long way off, but the edges have for a considerable time been lifting up away from adjacent parts of the earlier ridge (at one point it actually curled back on itself). The way this helps the application of half-coats is that the raised-up margin provides a stop that halts the swing of the brush and hence allows me to concentrate on the distribution of paint and direction of brushstrokes, without having to worry too much about paint spilling over the edge. This did once happen, some time ago, and the result was a drip of white paint that ran down over earlier accumulations of grey-and-white edges to a distance of about a third of an inch.

Many small accidental details are also unique to this piece: a drip of grey paint that fell inside the opened-up edge remained unnoticed till it dried and, of course, never got covered up with paint; the hair of a brush that got itself stuck in the edge; and some very small cracks that came about when I got a bad grip on the piece as I lifted it. The most conspicuous of these details, however, is a very narrow band of bright colours around the stalk end. I have explained in regard to other pieces that in the earlier stages I sometimes used to apply colour to the Thick Paintings: lobster colour to *Crouching Lobster*, green to *Lettuce* and, on one occasion, two half-coats of red to every piece I was working on. After that particular episode, I decided colour did not contribute very positively to the meaning of the Thick Paintings. This was before the area round the stem of *Alice's Rose* began to reveal rings of grey and white. There must be a layer of red somewhere deep inside it, but none of this is visible. The reason there is a band of colours ringing round the central core is that at one time I ran out of gesso and used some jars of regular acrylic paint I had been given by a friend, John Elderfield, who had been a student at Leeds University, where I once taught, and is now Director of Drawings at the Museum of Modern Art in New York. He gave me the jars of paint when he was about to return to England after an earlier period of work in America. There were several different colours, and the complex interplay of different hues gives a better indication of the actual structure of paint layers than the grey-and-white areas. Inside the narrow tunnel-like form that developed round the secondary break to the left of the bunch of leaves, the band of colours can also be seen with some difficulty. These are the only areas of coloured paint in any of the Thick Paintings.

Alice's Rose has been shown once only, in my *Et in Arcadia Id* installation at the Art Gallery of Nova Scotia in 1980. That was before the peripheral ridge had begun to open up. It was then shown with the side that I now regard as the underside facing up. This is the side on which the bulge around the bloom is more pronounced. Now that I rest it on that side when it is not in the process of being painted, that bulge causes one side to tilt diagonally upwards.

Alice's Rose has now accumulated 2397 half-coats of paint, as of July 28th, 1985. It measures twenty-one inches in length and fourteen inches across. Its height is just over five inches to the tip of the upraised side.

Danish Pastry (Plate XIX)

By the time I began work on *Danish Pastry*, I had had enough experience of other pieces painted with a No. 6 brush to anticipate the sort of breaking up of the surface that might be anticipated when paint was applied fairly loosely. I had decided I wanted to paint something that already had a texture like that to begin with, and when I saw the Danish pastry I realized it was just right. That was at a meeting of the Nova Scotia Confederation of University Faculty Associations that Vivian Cameron (no relation) and I organized at the College. My recollection is that I bought peanut-butter cookies and oatmeal cookies, and Vivian bought the Danish pastries, all as snacks to go with mid-morning and mid-afternoon coffee. It amounted to rather a lot for a dozen people, so there were some left.

Through the application of 2788 half-coats of paint, up to July 29th, 1985, *Danish Pastry* has largely fulfilled my original anticipations of it, and even though the particular bumps and bulges that originally covered the surface of the pastry have undoubtedly given way to others that are quite differently arranged, the general shape and character of the piece remains more true to the shape and character of its core subject than any other piece on which I have worked. As this particular kind of Danish pastry is rather amorphous, however, I doubt if many people would recognize it as such.

The piece did not retain its character without some coaxing on my part. Having observed the growth of tiny pimple-like forms around the area of overlap of half-coats in *Apple*, I had assumed every part of every Thick Painting painted with a No. 6 brush would eventually do the same. This was not the case. The top and base of *Beer Bottle*, for instance, became quite smooth as a result of the pressure of its own weight when resting on the bench, and this was what tended to happen with *Danish Pastry*. However, I adjusted the area of overlap of half-coats to run diagonally round the piece, and when it started to bulge in that area, I moved to the other diagonal. While each half-coat was drying, I rested it against a piece of wood to keep the wet paint off the bench. At the same time, I rather self-consciously applied paint loosely to the upper and lower surfaces in the hope of preserving as much of the original texture as possible and brushed out more vigorously the areas round the edge that showed a tendency to exaggerate the original texture.

Danish Pastry has been shown only once, in my installation *On -ing and Paint* in Regina in 1980. It now measures nine by eight and a half by five inches.

Chair (Plate XX)

This was the first new piece to be started after my return from England at the end of August 1979. It is also the first work whose history of painting I can vouch for with some measure of confidence, since the day I started it was also the day on which I began keeping fully systematic records (even though my working schedule would not be systematized in anything like its present form for many years to come). On September 23rd I applied two half-coats to it, as the two check marks under "23 S" indicate clearly. These should properly have been grey if I was to initiate a four half-coat cycle that would bring the piece to an all-white state. I added two more half-coats to complete the first cycle the next day. However, I worked slowly on the piece. It was by far the largest object I had attempted to paint, and even with the large No. 12 brush, the amount of work involved in carefully applying a half-coat of paint was quite intimidating. I think it probably took longer at first. As I work on pieces they tend to adapt to the swing of the brush, but the intricacies of a string-covered seat and of the fine struts joining the legs at the side were extremely difficult to negotiate. Because of the size, it was inconceivable I should attempt to paint it with anything smaller than the No. 12 brush, but its size only served to make negotiating smaller details still more difficult. It took till October 14th for me to work my way through four complete cycles (16 half-coats). I pushed that up to ninety-six half-coats by December 12th, but then set it aside till the middle of April. By June 16th, it had reached 124. On July 22nd, I added two half-coats; and then two more a week later. At the end of November, I added two half-coats two days apart; on December 13th, two more. The total then stood at 132, until October 10th, 1981, when I added two half-coats. Two days before Christmas I added two more, completing the cycle and bringing it back to an all-white state. I added four more half-coats in the middle of March 1982, but it was not until April 30th, when the average number of half-coats on all pieces was more than 1100, that I began to paint it — more or less — at the same rate as other pieces. As of July 29th, 1985, it has 1377 half-coats, having just received one grey half-coat. Tomorrow, I shall add three more to complete the cycle.

One of the considerations, when I decided to paint the chair, was the tradition of chairs in art. I thought of Van Gogh, but more especially of Robert Rauschenberg's *Pilgrim* and Joseph Kosuth's *One and Three Chairs*, because they involved actual chairs in association with pictures. I also thought of Plato's couch, and decided the closest I could come to it in practice was a dining-room chair.

The particular chair was a Danish design, one of a set of six my wife and I had bought in England shortly after we were married in 1962, but they were also available in Canada. Sue and Roald Nasgaard, whom we had known since Roald worked with me at Guelph, had bought the same chair, and they still have them looking as good as new in their apartment in Toronto. But then, Sue and Roald Nasgaard do not have any children. My daughter, Matilda, used to rock back and forward on the chair I eventually painted, until she went over backwards and landed in a heap on the floor. She escaped unhurt, the way children (almost) always do, but the back of the chair snapped away from the seat at one side. We got that mended, but the string seat soon began to give way at the front and nobody in Leeds or Toronto seemed to be able to fix that. When I started to paint it, I stapled the broken strings into place, and after a few coats of paint, all the elegance of form that had attracted us to the chairs in the first place seemed to have returned. The photograph in the booklet that I produced from my *Keeping Marlene out of the Picture — and Lawn* installation at the Anna Leonowens Gallery in the fall of 1980 gives a very good idea of this early stage of its development. It had then accumulated 128 half-coats, but the form of the chair was still very much as new, lean and refined in structure and curvilinear design alike.

The struts between the legs at the side were only an inch away from the base of the seat and, recalling what had happened with *Alarm Clock* and several other pieces since, I thought it quite possible that space would eventually fill in. But the back was composed of a single five-inch-wide backrest fitted to two slender supports at the side, carved from the same pieces of wood as the back legs; the space between the seat and backrest measured fifteen and a half by nine inches. I found it inconceivable that that space should ever fill in. After 1377 half-coats, however, far fewer than I have applied to many other pieces, that space has been reduced to ten and a half by four inches. The struts between the legs merged a long time ago into the generally increasing bulk of the seat. The general shape is still chair-like, but the character of the form has utterly changed. Every member is visually heavy and bulky, and the piece is physically very heavy. I am no longer able to lift it, but I can still topple it forward, allowing it to rest with the front of the seat and the back resting on the floor, while I paint the underside of the seat and the legs, which stick up diagonally into the air. From the start, I had made the overlap of half-coats come round the edge of the seat. The way the paint accumulated at the front and back, however, was different from the growth at the sides. At front and back the overlap resulted in the slow emergence of a rounded two-inch-broad slab, which has never shown any inclination to sharpen into a ridge, while double ridges of quite flamboyant form have pushed out to each side. The differentiation must have been influenced by the way I paint from side to side across the forms. It is fortunate the front has not developed a ridge, as that would have made it impossible to rock it forward over that area to paint the underside. The texture of the string seat disappeared a long time ago, but a quite distinct ripple effect, with rather large undulations, has emerged along the inside curve of the backrest. Slightly bulbous growths have emerged round the feet (undifferentiated in the chair itself), presumably the result of pressure causing the paint to spread outwards.

Lettuce (Plate XXI)

Form was always a consideration in selecting objects to paint. The form of the chair had appealed to me because of its openness; it seemed inconceivable it would ever be engulfed in a single block of paint. I was attracted to the lettuce for exactly opposite reasons. As a roughly spherical object of a fair size, it should allow me to shift the area of overlap of half-coats almost indefinitely and hence avoid altogether the growth of ridges. But there was another reason I wanted to paint it that had nothing to do with form. As a student living on my own in a rather cramped apartment in England, I had always found the provision of food and planning of meals rather a problem. Part of the problem was that it took me a long time to eat something like a lettuce. The incident I have in mind concerned a lettuce I had bought, put in a cupboard and forgotten. Two weeks later, I opened the cupboard to find dark brown liquid spreading out over the bottom of the shelf. I do not recall that anything else remained of the lettuce at all. I wanted to paint a lettuce now because I believed it would disintegrate completely within the shell of paint.

That meant, of course, that I would have to work very quickly indeed, if I was to build up a sufficiently strong shell of paint to hold the piece together once the process of disintegration began. I was enabled to do this by the use of my wife's hair dryer to dry off each application of paint immediately after it was made. I started the piece on October 2nd. My wife and I drove down to Sobey's after lunch to buy the lettuce (she may have wanted other things as well), and I began to paint it as soon as we got back. I applied fourteen half-coats that day, but the next day I must have been busy with something else because I applied only two half-coats, and none at all to any other piece. Within a few days, however, I was painting twenty, forty, fifty, and eventually seventy-six half-coats on October 21st, while other pieces were largely set aside. By that date, the total had risen to 520, and it passed the one thousand mark less than a month later. Only gradually did I begin to divide my attention between it and other pieces, so that when it passed the two thousand mark on June 11th, it was more than one thousand half-coats ahead of any other piece.

I chose to buy the lettuce from Sobey's because I liked the way they wrapped them, at that time, with a piece of waxed paper and rubber band. That choice may have increased the initial difficulties, because I remember distinctly how hard it was to get paint to stick to the waxed paper. Once it had stuck, that area was the least trouble, because the waxed paper would not decay and would not be effected by any moisture that might emerge from the lettuce. But it did take a considerable effort to completely cover that waxed paper. Even then, I remember one corner must have got caught somehow and turned upwards, creating a projection on the surface that was clearly distinguishable for more than a year afterwards.

The first indication of decomposition was the evident withering of stalk area of the lettuce in the gap left by the waxed paper. That must only have been four or five days into the piece, since I clearly recall the image of the withered stalk beneath a skin of paint that had not yet grown thick enough to conceal details of its form. This undoubtedly prompted me to increase the pace in the days that followed, but in spite of this, a crack appeared a few days later along one edge of the waxed paper. It was a deep crack, going right through the paint layer to the surface of the lettuce itself and causing some real anxiety, since it was in a position where decomposing material could spill out and ruin the piece. I redoubled my efforts again, and happily, the crack sealed over and did not reappear. The paint layer was now sufficiently thick that the detailed form of the lettuce was no longer visible.

It may have been another week after that, that the lettuce began to liquefy. I could hear it slopping around inside as I turned the piece over, and I wondered how it would stand up. In fact, it stood up very well, but I became aware that the area around the stalk not covered by the waxed paper was beginning to cave in. The liquid was evidently seeping out and evaporating through the only part that the wax paper would allow it to escape. There were no signs of cracking even as the stalk turned most steeply in. Moisture was just permeating the skin of gesso itself, allowing the vegetable inside to dehydrate. When the concavity reached its maximum depth, it seemed as though there could be no room for anything else inside the doubled-up shell of paint, but I have always imagined there would be a thin, dark brown, solid core of decomposed material between the two layers of paint, in addition, of course, to the waxed paper and rubber band.

By this time, there was no longer a sound of sloshing liquid when I turned the work over. It was finally stable, and I confronted the new task of restoring its distorted form to approximate the rough sphere from which I had started. This proved rather easier than I might have anticipated. I was able to speed the natural tendency for concavities to fill in by adjusting the area of overlap of half-coats, and before too many months had gone by, I was able to shift my attention to more subtle adjustments of formal balance.

From the start, I worked on *Lettuce* with the middle-sized No. 8 brush. I have never set any particular pattern for the application of brushstrokes, and I have applied the paint very directly, only brushing out places where the paint was obviously too thick, and even then only until the distribution was more even, not until the surface was smooth or the markings conformed to any particular alignment. I have generally not allowed the application to become as loose as with *Apple* or *Danish Pastry* or the sides of *Beer Bottle*. There was one quite brief period, maybe near the end of the first year, when I became aware I was trying to force the growth by piling the paint on too thickly, but I was uncomfortable with the results and have never been tempted away from my established routine subsequently. The fact that I work on *Lettuce* in the darkest corner of my studio also helps to keep my brushwork relaxed and unselfconscious.

That very loose handling is something that seems to work only with a No. 6 brush and then only with certain sorts of surfaces. The densely bulging and buckling relief that it produces is also quite different in character from the more politely curved cobblestones that the No. 8 brush generates when used moderately freely. These too can become quite dense, but they generally seem to lie more evenly on the surface and show less tendency to group into the complex convexities and concavities that are particularly conspicuous on the sides of *Beer Bottle.*

As I continued to work, and as the paint built up and the weight increased, *Lettuce* was the first piece to reveal the flattening out of forms against the bench. What I am talking about here is not the sort of retarding of the development of surface irregularities that has kept the top and bottom of *Beer Bottle* smooth, but an altogether more drastic flattening out of forms already developed, leaving a glossy patch in the area of contact with the plastic and a linear imprint from the corrugated-paper padding underneath. Once I became aware this was happening, I was able to use it as a means of encouraging a generally spherical contour.

As of July 30th, 1985, *Lettuce* has acquired 4036 half-coats of paint, still more than nine hundred ahead of any other piece. It has been shown twice, in my *(to be continued)* installations at A Space in 1982 and 1985. On both occasions, people said they could still detect something of the texture of the original lettuce through all that paint. I, naturally, explained that the lettuce was wrapped in waxed paper and a rubber band when I started, so those are the textures they should be able to detect if the original object really could still have any influence on the present surface of the work. Nonetheless, I find the response interesting.

It has occurred to me since I started to work on *Lettuce*, that its subject represents a minor iconographic innovation. In the story of *Rapunzel*, according to one version, Rapunzel's mother became pregnant after eating lettuce stolen from a neighbour's garden. Carol Duncan, when she visited the College, expressed the view that this was because lettuce was considered an aphrodisiac. However, I found this inconsistent with the fact that lettuce had a soporific effect on the Flopsy Bunnies. I know of no reference to the lettuce in poetry and do not recall a single painting of that vegetable.

Matilda's Chestnut (Plate XXII)

My daughter, Matilda, was six years old when we returned to Canada, and at that time we were very close. When she saw me painting my Thick Paintings in my basement studio, she wanted to join in. So I suggested she should choose an object that I would paint for her and she could join in the painting of that piece. The object she chose was a horse-chestnut, and we started painting it with a No. 8 brush on October 6th. I have worked on it steadily since then. I cannot pretend I was really surprised when she showed very little interest in painting once I had a Thick Painting she was allowed to work on. She may have contributed as many as four or five half-coats to a total which now stands at 2847, according to my records.

The No. 8 brush was actually rather large for painting the chestnut at first, and I do remember that it had a somewhat irregular form to begin with. As time went on, and I kept changing the location of areas of overlap of half-coats, it became more regular, but it has tended to produce a number of flattish planes around its surface, rather than a more properly spherical form, and it has revealed no more than a hint of the "cobblestone" effect, which is so pronounced on some other No. 8 brush pieces. Those flattish areas over the surface give the piece a quite distinctive character and seem naturally to endow the moderately worked brushstrokes with a distinctive character too. They have also been useful from a practical point of view, because it is easier to balance this piece on the bench than, for instance, *Lettuce*, which has had to be propped up with three half-bricks. *Matilda's Chestnut* has been shown only once, in the *Keeping Marlene out of the Picture — and Lawn* installation at the Anna Leonowens Gallery in October 1980. It was then quite small; it is now seven inches across.

I have always considered the three pieces I am painting that bear the names of my children — *Matilda's Chestnut, Edwin's Egg,* and *Gregory's Present* — to be their property. However, I will continue to paint them as long as I can. Other pieces are available for sale and hence may, in theory, be taken out of the range of my brush at any moment. These three pieces are not; and it was, therefore, important that the core object should be small, so as to delay as long as possible the time when they would become too cumbersome to handle.

Light (Plate XXIII)

The light was a yellow goose-neck desk lamp that had belonged to my second son, Edwin, while we were in Guelph, but had gone with me to Halifax. I had thought of painting it before I left for England in June 1979, but I waited because it had belonged to Edwin, and we bought him another one to replace it. I liked the idea of painting "light," but I also wanted to make a Thick Painting that would not merge into a single blob of paint. It is no coincidence that *Light* and *Chair* were started within a few days of each other.

Light proved very awkward to paint. It was a problem applying paint inside the lampshade and round the bulb. The brush was really too large for the goose-neck, which I painted all at once within the same half-coat, but which somehow managed to develop four vertical ridges with four concave areas in between. I experimented with several ways of dealing with the six-foot-long cord before finally accepting that it had to be allotted six continuous feet of bench space, and I had difficulty balancing it to paint the underside. Moreover, as I persevered, the form developed all sorts of gratuitous complexities, that seemed to reflect not so much the form-generating properties of the process as the intricacies of shape of the original object. Of course, that was the main reason I had chosen that particular object, but when I saw the results I was very dissatisfied. I continued for some time, notwithstanding, and became increasingly dissatisfied. As the lampshade got clogged up with paint, it became very heavy, and the goose-neck proved not to be strong enough to sustain it. Suddenly it would collapse forward and flop down onto the bench. When I showed it at the Centre for Art Tapes late in 1980, I avoided the problem of balance by attaching the square base vertically to the wall and allowing the cable and the actual light on its goose-neck to hang under their own weight. But the decision had already been made. The title of that installation, *Chrysalis*, referred to the fact that I had already made the first incision through the paint layer and had begun to pull it back to reveal the yellow enamel of the lampshade underneath.

When the piece came back to my studio early in December, I relented, sealed up the incision, and applied a hundred more half-coats before finally bracing myself to the task of removing the paint. Rather selfconsciously using a penknife that had belonged to my father, I cut through the paint and slowly pried it away from the lampshade (both inside and out), from the goose-neck, and from the square base on which it had once stood. In some places I was pleased to find how readily the gesso peeled away from the surface, and I was especially pleased that the light bulb survived intact. But in other places, I had to pick at it a centimetre at a time. There were spots where pieces of gesso resolutely clung to the surface, and others where it peeled away the yellow enamel from the metal; and there were patches of rust on the goose-neck, but no serious damage. The gesso had proved very tough to cut through, and it had been a slow process. My records show a gap from March 20th, 1981, when it had reached 457 half-coats, to October 10th, when I added five half-coats to the part that remained and started *Residue Plus Penknife.*

What remained was the six-foot-long cable, the only part that had seemed to me expressive of the natural principle of growth within the process. I had made the division of half-coats coincide with its edges, so ridges developed on either side. When I showed it at the Centre for Art Tapes, it was about two inches wide, but ironically,

this was the part that suffered the most serious damage to befall any of my Thick Paintings thus far. When moved slowly the gesso is quite flexible, at least for some time after its application, and it certainly proved extraordinarily tough when I tried to cut it with a knife, but it is evidently quite fragile when struck with a sudden blow. I stood on it, and it cracked right across. It was still held together by the cable, and I placed it so the two sides were properly matched up. I do not believe anybody noticed the crack during the show and, happily, when I got it back to my studio, every trace disappeared after less than half a dozen further coats, and there were a hundred more half-coats before I finally started to strip away the paint from every other part.

At that time, the strip of paint round the cable may have been three inches wide and less than three quarters of an inch thick along most of the length of the cable, but it bulged out at the point where it fitted into the back of the square yellow base supporting the goose-neck. I was pleased that removing the paint from the lamp proper had still left the section round the cord firmly stuck to the back of that square yellow base, and I allowed myself to hope the join would remain stable. My method of working, from then on, involved placing the painted cord along the low bench on which I worked, with the unpainted yellow lamp right at the end. When it was in this position, I would paint one side of the cable. When I turned it over, I let the goose-neck hang over the edge, and the lampshade then came to rest on a piece of styrofoam that I had placed on the basement floor to prevent it from getting scraped. I had to paint very carefully around the end nearest the lamp but was able to swing the brush back and forth more rhythmically as I painted along the length of the cord (and over the plug at the end) while sitting sideways on the edge of the bench.

As time went by, the paint round the cord expanded and eventually grew beyond the edges of the square yellow base to which it was attached. As it developed beyond that point, it lifted up the lamp itself, which then became an appendage to the cable. The ribbon of paint just in front of that yellow square had developed in a somewhat twisted form because of the way it had been painted in the very early stages, and this twist became exaggerated by something in the process that made the side of the cord further away from me accumulate paint more thickly and also made the ridge nearer to me dip downward. The result of all this was that the lamp, suspended on the edge of the block of paint, was tipped quite steeply to the right as I looked at it from in front, and I kept finding myself having to make it tip even further (wedging it with rolled-up pieces of paper underneath) so as to stop the nearer ridge from coming into contact with the bench as I worked. Eventually, I realized I could correct the tendency of the nearer ridge to dip down by running my finger underneath it to remove any surplus of wet paint, but by then, as I say, the tilt of the lamp was already quite steep. The paint round the six-foot length of the cord was also getting quite heavy. I could no longer lift it, but I could still drag it towards me and then roll it over onto the other side. I tried to make this movement as smooth as possible, hanging onto the goose-neck of the lamp so as not to let it crash against the styrofoam pad, but it always went the last few inches with a thud. It was to be expected that jolting around would put some strain on the joint between the lamp proper and the slab of paint around the cord. One day it snapped. The lamp was still held on by the cord, but it just hung limply forward and obstinately resisted all my efforts to glue it back in place.

As the paint round the cord had grown beyond the edges of the square yellow base, I painted each half-coat only as far as the line of the back of the yellow base. That left an expanding open edge of exposed streaks of grey and white, rather like the edges of *Alice's Rose*. They seemed to make sense in relation to the totality of the piece, but as successive attempts to glue that base back in place failed, I had to brace myself to the only way of proceeding that seemed to offer any prospect of a lasting solution. I carefully wedged that yellow square in position with blocks of wood, then added a continuous half-coat up to a line, which I drew very carefully about an inch in front of the place where the goose-neck connected with the square yellow base and then back, skirting the bottom of the goose-neck over the rear portion of the yellow base. I allowed a considerable amount of gesso to flow down behind, then painted over all those exposed strata of grey-and-white paint, and proceeded to paint the areas that would normally have been covered by that half-coat. Remembering how I had eventually managed to deal with the mackerel, I repeated those same applications over a period of several days before venturing to turn it over and resume the normal sequence of half-coats.

Very soon the paint was building up quite thickly along the new boundary, and the characteristic pattern of grey-and-white striations was again building up. As layer after layer of paint covered the irregular vertical face of the old boundary, its forms found a new integration, and the now quite huge slab of paint around the cable continued to grow. There are complexities of form around the base of the lamp that make it clear a final resolution has not yet emerged, but that is not necessarily a bad thing, as the sense of structural development is visually coherent as transitional form.

The slab of paint round the cord of *Light* is now thirteen inches across and three and a half inches deep. The line along the edge of the ridges is remarkably straight, doubtless due to the effect of repeatedly resting it briefly on the edge as I turn it over.

Edwin's Egg (Plate XXIV)

It was obviously more than coincidence that I should begin to produce a Thick Painting for Edwin on the same day I had begun to use his desk lamp as the basis of another, but I do not recall there was any explicit trade-off. I was very pleased when he asked me to paint the egg for him. I did point out that I was already working on another egg, but that was what he wanted, so of course I agreed. There was never any suggestion, as with Matilda, that he should participate in its production.

To differentiate *Edwin's Egg* from the other *Egg*, I made the line of overlap of half-coats fall diagonally across the egg, but kept turning the piece between each pair of half-coats so that it always came in a different position, though the angle of the diagonal was always more or less the same. There was no problem about wet paint coming in contact with the bench, because the curvature of the egg lifted it up just enough to avoid that. Whereas the first *Egg* developed to form points at each end, *Edwin's Egg* slowly began to flatten out at the ends, as a ring some distance from each end began to lift up, in the area where the diagonal lines of overlap tended to fall most consistently. The form the piece took on could well be described as barrel-like. It tended to follow naturally that the ends of the barrel came to be painted quite loosely and have taken on a characteristic lumpiness, while the sides, under the intermittent pressure of the work's own weight, have remained smoother, inviting a more vigorous brushing out of paint. Over that surface, brushstrokes run from end to end, just like the staves of a barrel, but the sides and ends are much more fully integrated in this piece than, for instance, in *Beer Bottle*.

Edwin's Egg has now claimed a total of 2683 half-coats and is eight and a half inches long and seven inches in diameter. It has been shown only once, in the same exhibition at the Centre for Art Tapes, which also included the work based on Edwin's table lamp, *Light*.

Gregory's Present (Plate XXV)

The present was from my elder son, Gregory, to me. Both he and I remember it as a box of Maynard's Wine Gums, though I seem to recall the beaming boy's face with bulging cheek on a yellow background that actually belongs to Rowntree's Clear Gums. (It hardly seems possible he should have put one kind of candy in the other sort of box?) He had sent them to me through the mail — all neatly wrapped — from England, several months before I began the Thick Paintings. They were not a birthday present or anything like that. He just decided I would like them, and of course I was very touched. I ate most of them, but kept two in the box. Once I had started to paint the chestnut for Matilda and the egg for Edwin, I obviously wanted to produce a Thick Painting for Gregory as well, and this memento was an equally obvious choice.

In painting *Gregory's Present*, I have consistently tried to maintain its rectangular form by adjusting the area of overlap of half-coats. This has sometimes necessitated diagonal divisions extending over parts of both larger sides. It has, therefore, been necessary to prop it up on a half-brick, which has left indentations on each side, but has also released the pressure from those longer sides, allowing a denser pattern of "cobblestones" to develop than on any other piece painted with a No. 8 brush. All three pieces painted for my children were at first done with a No. 6 brush, but all changed together to a No. 8 brush on October 10th, 1981. Apart from the time when they have been away on exhibition, I have always painted the three pieces in step. It is no coincidence that they have thus far been shown once each, in the three Halifax exhibitions I had in the fall of 1980. *Gregory's Present* went to *Et in Arcadia Id* at the Art Gallery of Nova Scotia. Unfortunately it was the one work that did not show up in the booklets I later produced using photographs from these installations.

Gregory's Present now has 2628 half-coats as of July 21st, 1985. It measures nine by seven and a half by five inches. From the start, I have always applied grey gesso in brushstrokes running across the longer side and white half-coats in brushstrokes running along them, resulting in a characteristic grid texture of perpendicularly intersecting striations.

Identified Object (Plate XXVI)

I have referred in several places to choices I made in relation to particular pieces, specifically so as to differentiate them from the rest. Mainly, this has been a matter of formal differentiation, but I also wanted to differentiate them in other ways too, as much for the sake of making those ways an issue in the body of work as a whole as for further differentiating the piece concerned. Hence, there is one piece from which I have withheld paint for some time, one in which the larger part of the object is unpainted, one that is paint all the way through, and three that are not offered for sale. I now decided there should be one piece whose title did not indicate the object at its core, nor would I reveal what that object was. After some hesitation I settled on the title *Identified Object*, because that title itself provided an identity for it.

From the start, I worked on this piece with a No. 12 brush, and I followed a clearly preconceived system. From time to time, I fix on a new line of junction (rather than overlap) of half-coats, and I mark it out with brushing over the paint just inside it to cause the liquid bulge to rise up along the edge, thus speeding the development of ridges. When a particular ridge has become sufficiently formed, I move to another section, selecting it so as to encourage a generally spherical contour. The pattern of intersecting ridges, in varying stages of merging into the mass of the piece, has often seemed to suggest the rib forms of a Gothic vault turned inside out.

I started painting *Identified Object* on October 10th, 1981. I have now applied 2322 half-coats. The piece measures nine and a half inches in diameter. It has not, as yet, been exhibited.

Residue Plus Penknife (Plate XXVII)

The paint peeled off *Light* as a tough, leathery skin somewhat less than half an inch thick. Since that represented an accumulation of more than two hundred layers, it is hardly surprising that the existence of those layers was not discernable with the naked eye. It did not look at all like the exposed edges of paint layers in *Alice's Rose* or *Light* itself, as it was later to develop. It came off in chunks of varying size, as well as some tiny fragments. It would have gone against the grain to throw it away, so I parcelled it up, together with that penknife of my father's that I had used to remove it, in a plastic bag from a Dominion store (it could have been I.G.A. or Sobey's), and I fastened the whole securely with Scotch tape, shaping it into as regular a form as I could manage.

I began to paint it with a No. 12 brush on October 10th, 1980, the same day on which I resumed work on *Light* itself and on which I began *Identified Object*. I worked on it from the start with a No. 12 brush and, from the start also, I determined to brush the paint out as vigorously as possible, so as to round out the form to the maximum extent. Although it had the kind of shape that might have allowed me to turn it at a wide range of angles, I have always rested it on the original top and bottom, and have avoided the formation of ridges by moving the area of overlap of half-coats up and down over the considerable length at the sides. When I eventually settled into a routine, I found it best to make all the brushstrokes go in the same direction in any particular half-coat, but I would change their angle from one half-coat to the next. Usually, however, I would find it necessary to finish off the edge of the half-coat with brushstrokes running horizontally round the central area of the piece. The result has been that that area of the surface has developed with a more horizontal articulation of low eliptical bulges and shallow depressions than elsewhere on the piece. Because I have always brushed out the paint so vigorously, the surface undulations have become quite subtle and, for the same reason, the mesh of intersecting brushmarks is extremely fine, not at all like those on *Gregory's Present*.

Residue Plus Penknife has been shown only once, at Eye Level Gallery in one of my *(to be continued)* installations, in January 1983. It has now accumulated 1594 half-coats and is ten and a quarter inches high, ten and a half inches long and eight and a half inches wide.

Since October 10th, 1981, I have started no more new Thick Paintings.

A Final Note

The collection of anecdotes, reminiscences, and rationalizations given in this appendix might well be extended a good deal further. All of it is relevant to the work, and I would wish people to come to the work with as much understanding of it as possible. But all of it is most significant when specific details are subsumed under a general awareness of the forces involved in a process of growth. I may speculate that these forces are partly of a physical nature, resulting from my physical activity in relation to the physical stuff with which I work; but partly also of a psychological nature, the result of my judgment, whether conscious or spontaneous, of what is right (or "inevitable") for those particular forms. Both aspects speak of the world, the first directly, since the stuff of my art is continuous with the stuff of the material world; the second indirectly, through the way a sensibility evident in the work has been shaped by lived experience.

List of Plates

The figure in parentheses gives the total number of half-coats of paint accumulated by the given date; it also corresponds to the status of the work at the time the plate was made. The page reference indicates where a discussion of the work can be found. All works collection of the artist, except *Alice's Rose,* collection of Glenbow Museum, Calgary.

Plates

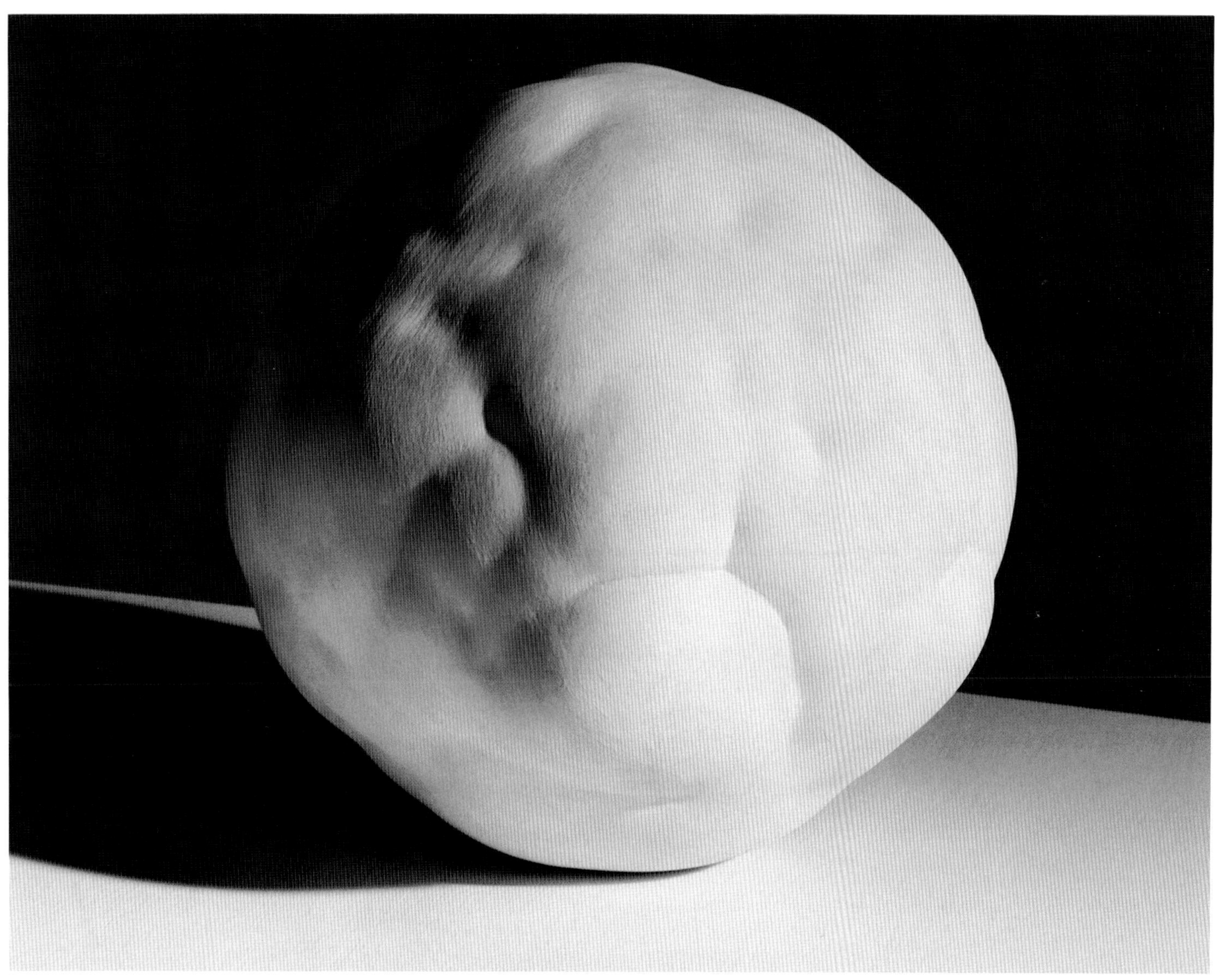

I

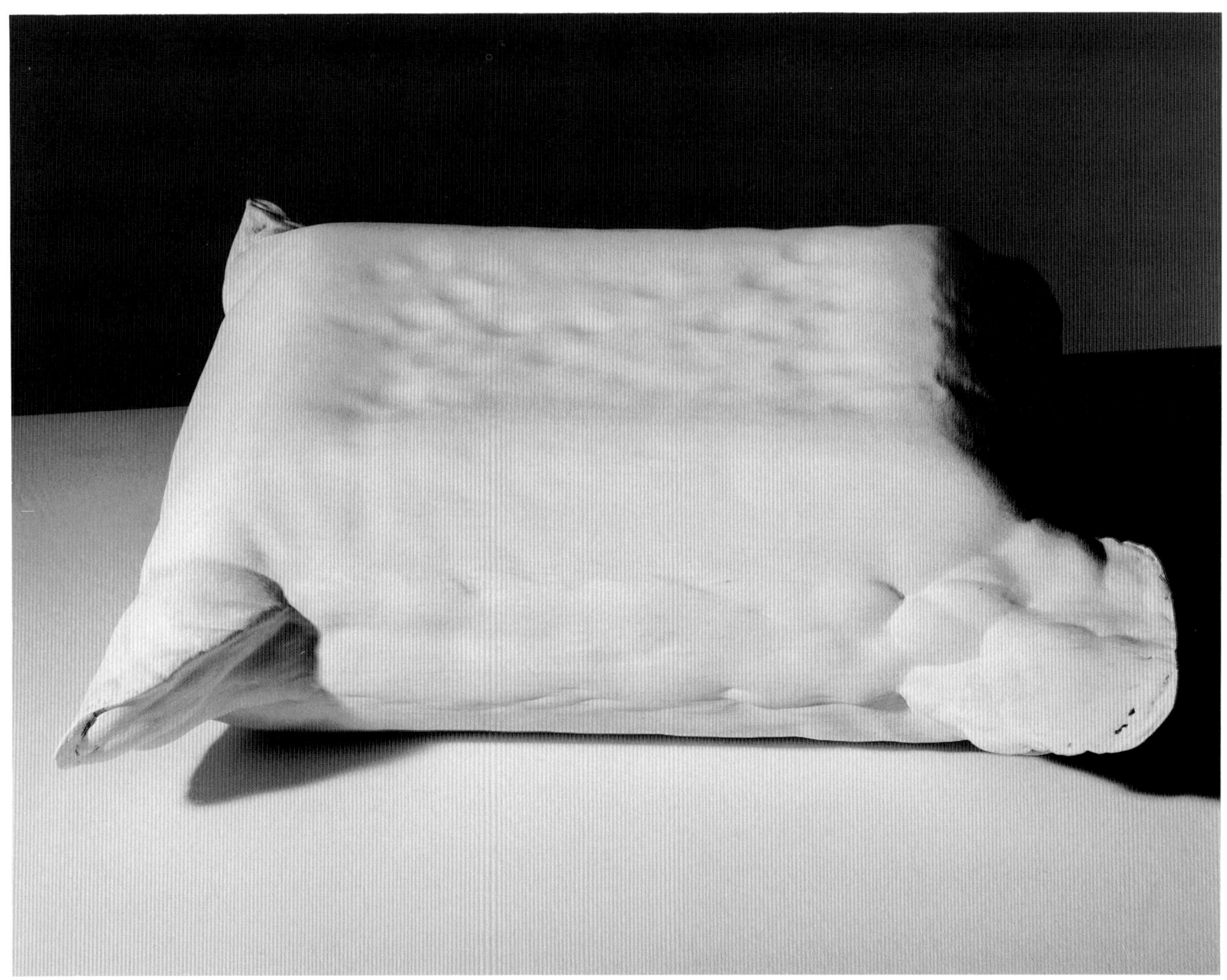

II

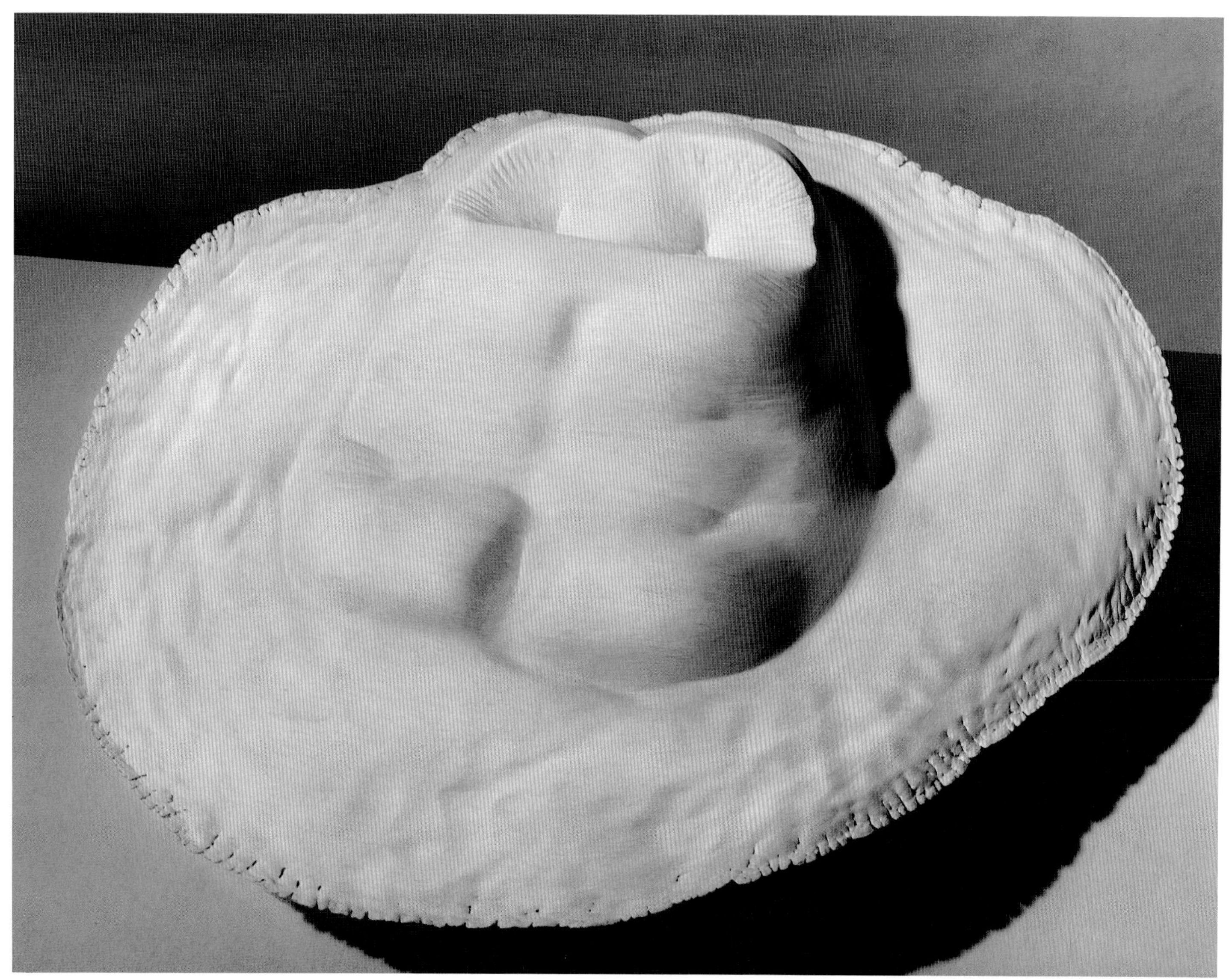

III

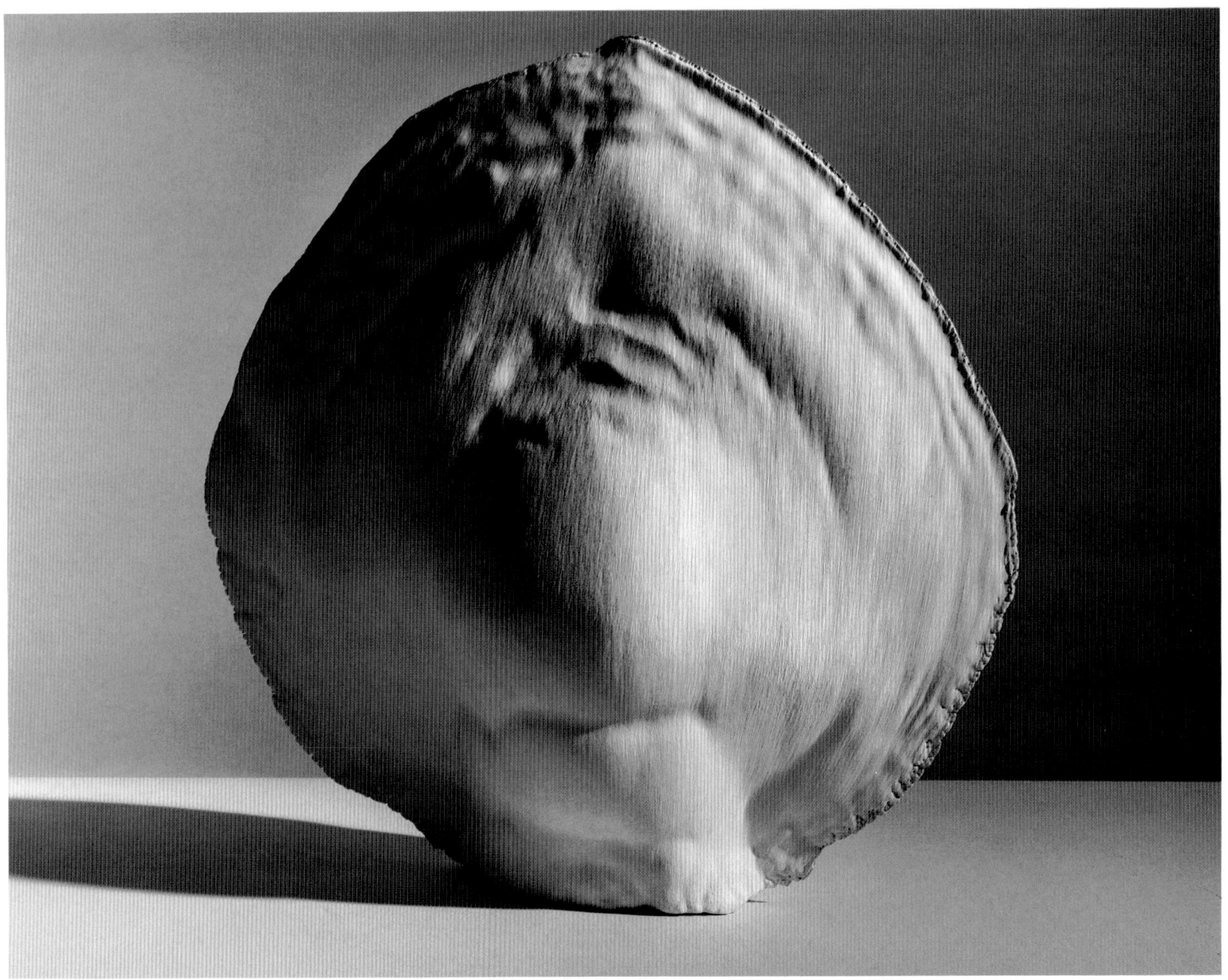

IV

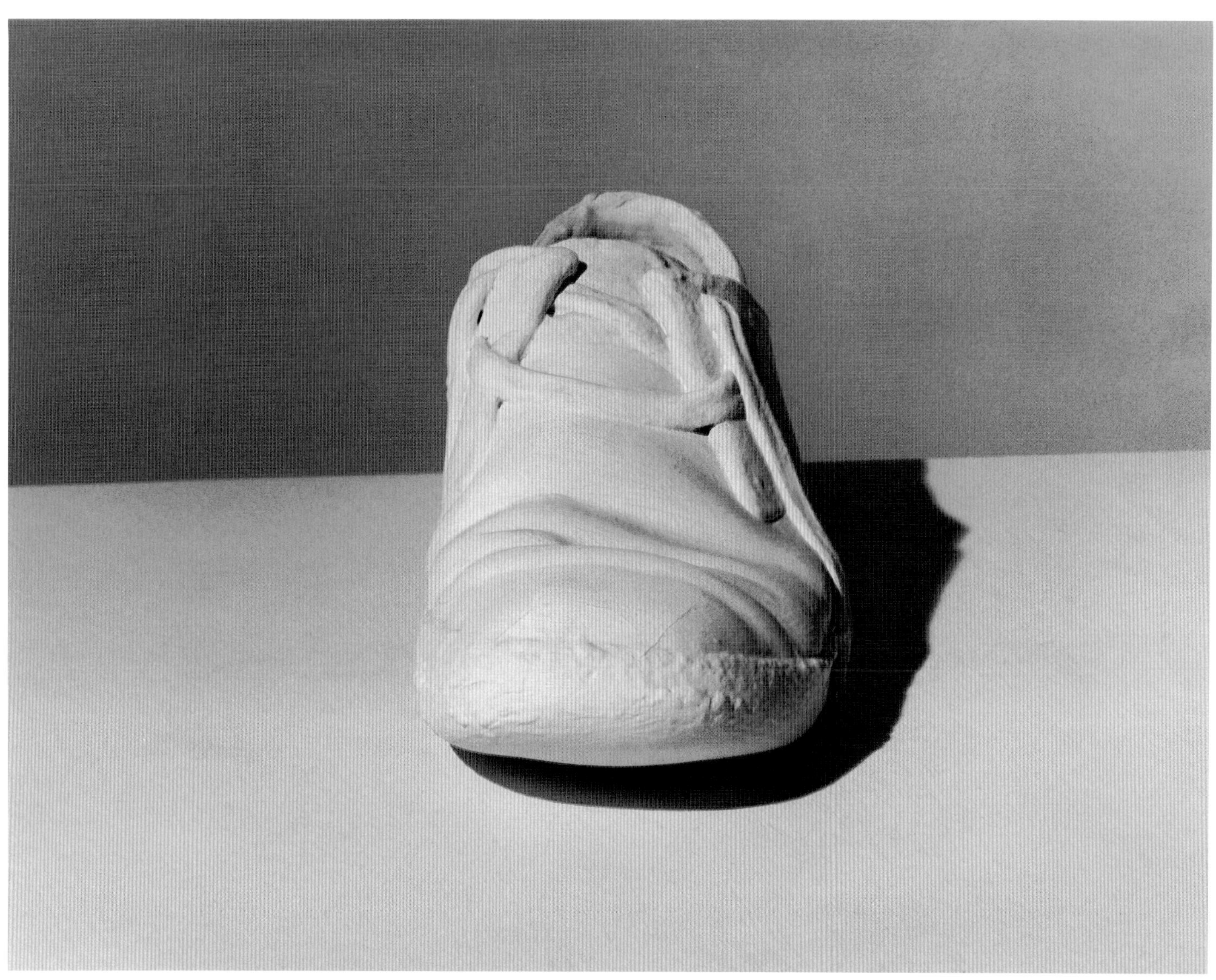

V

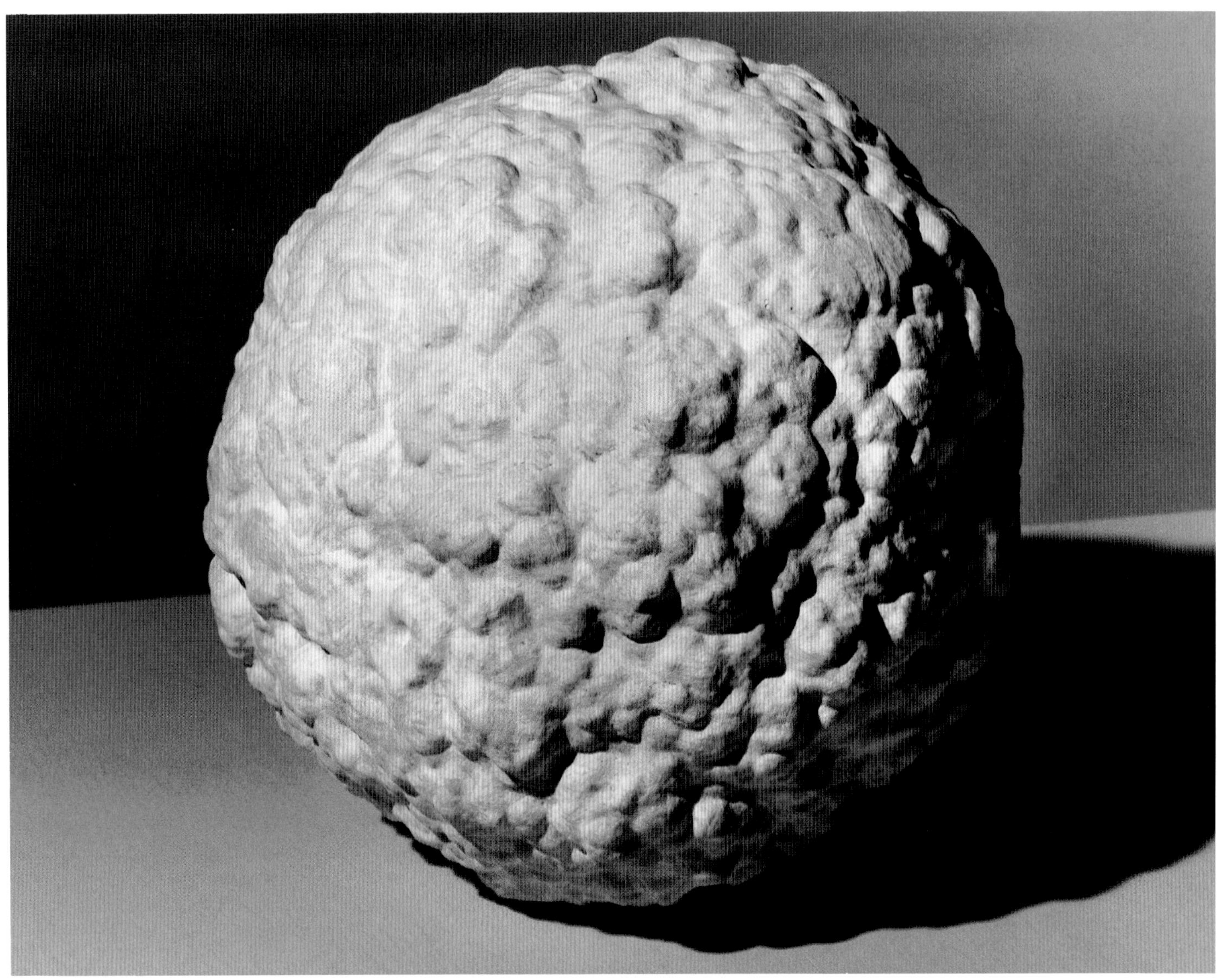

VI

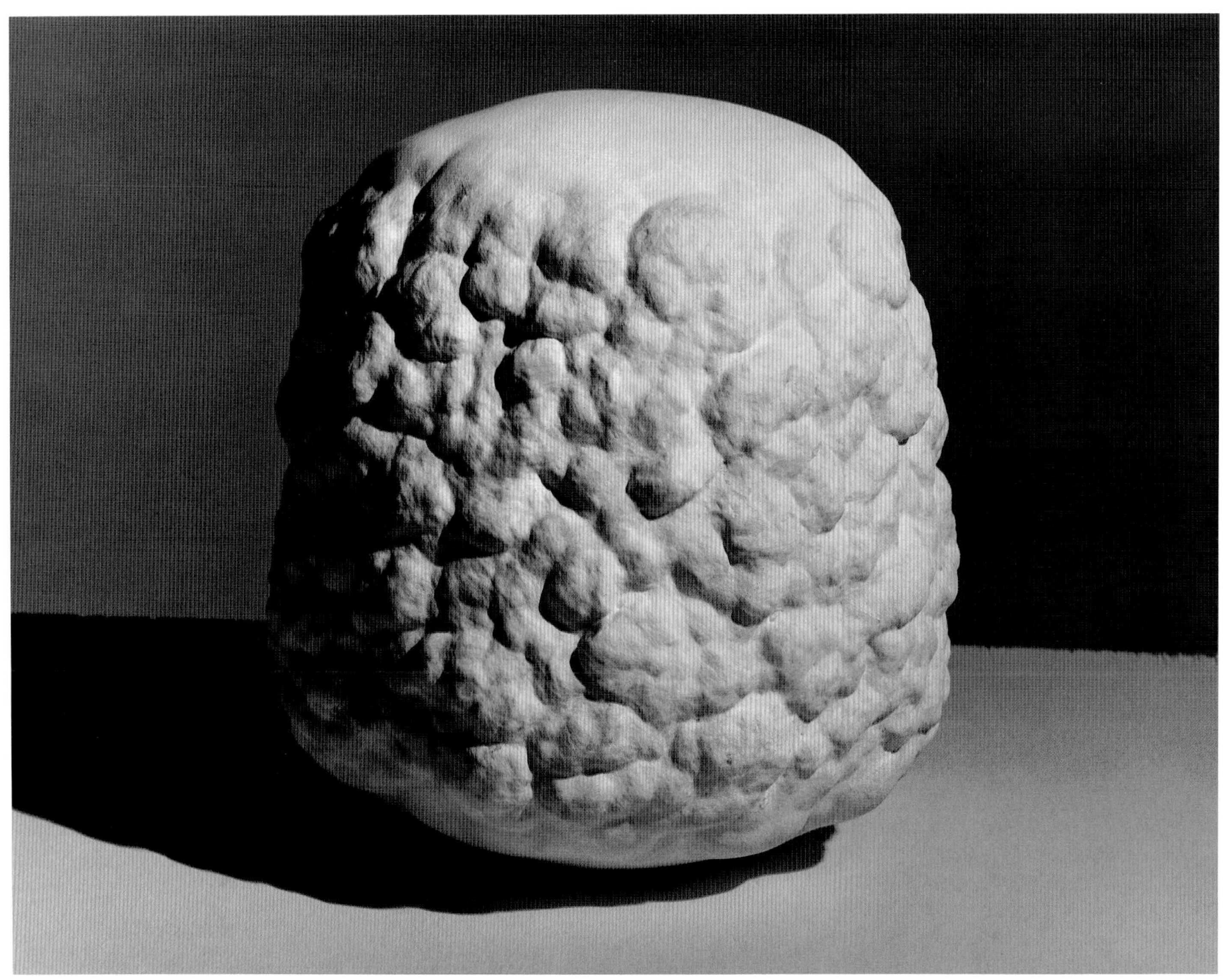

VII

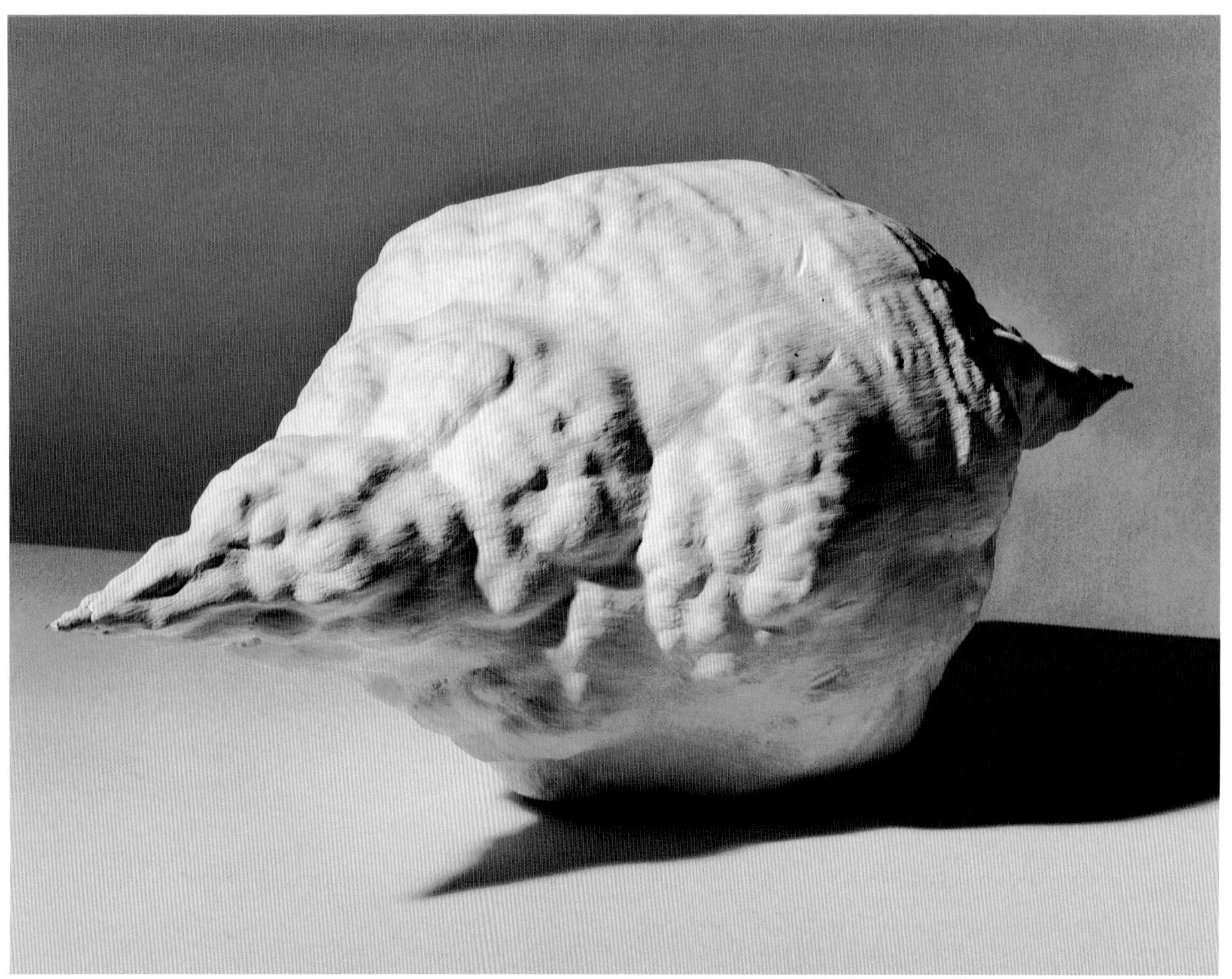

VIII

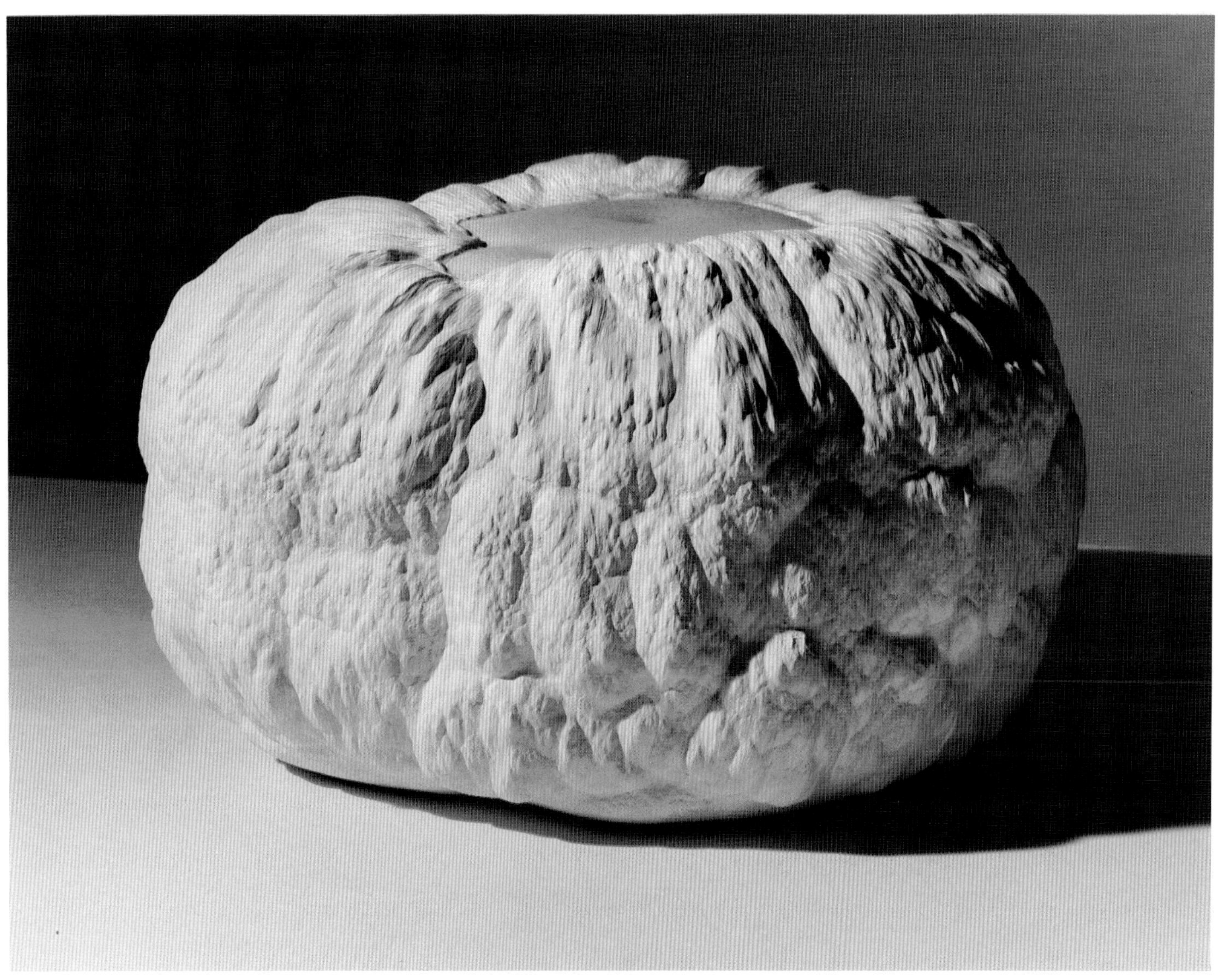

IX

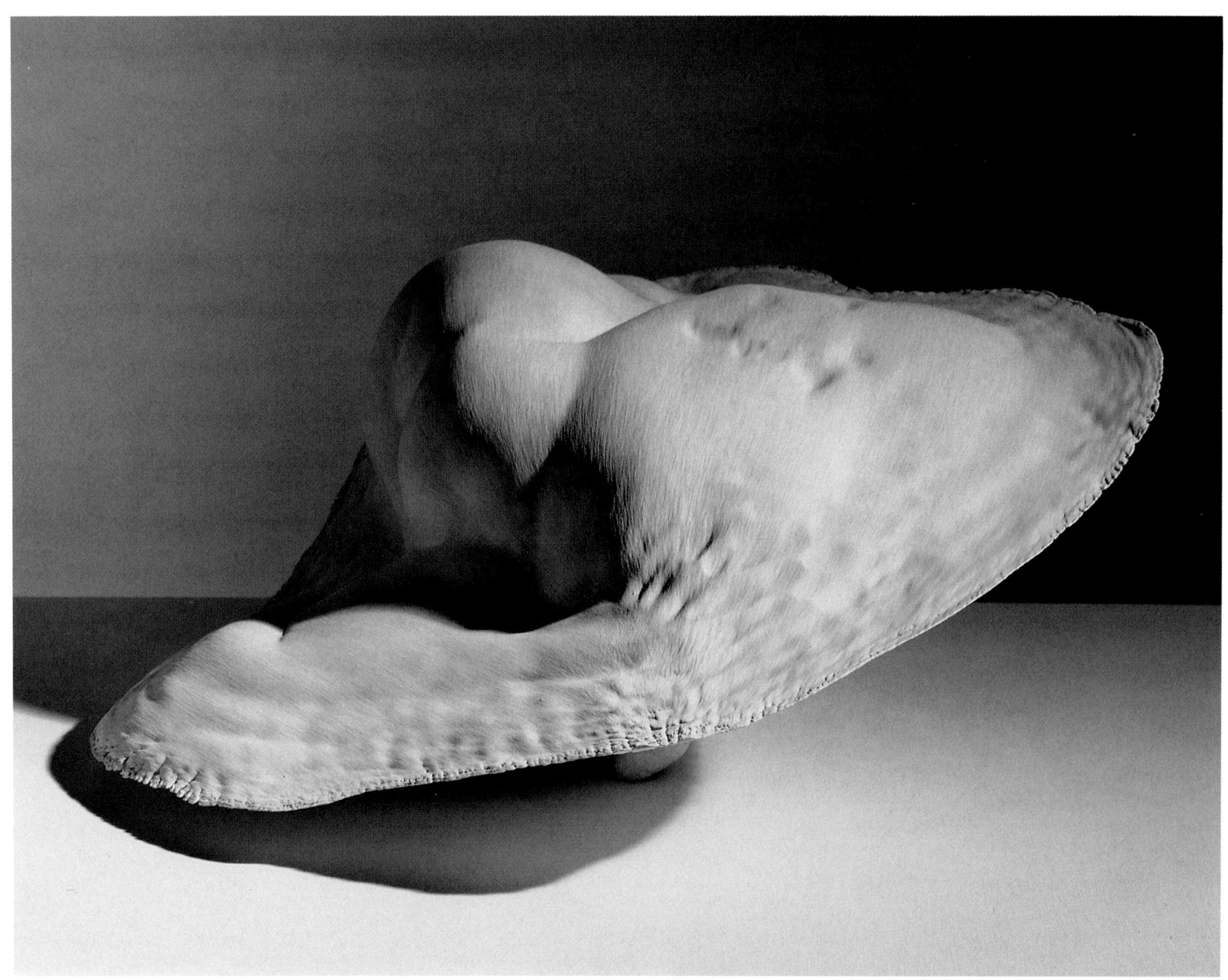

X

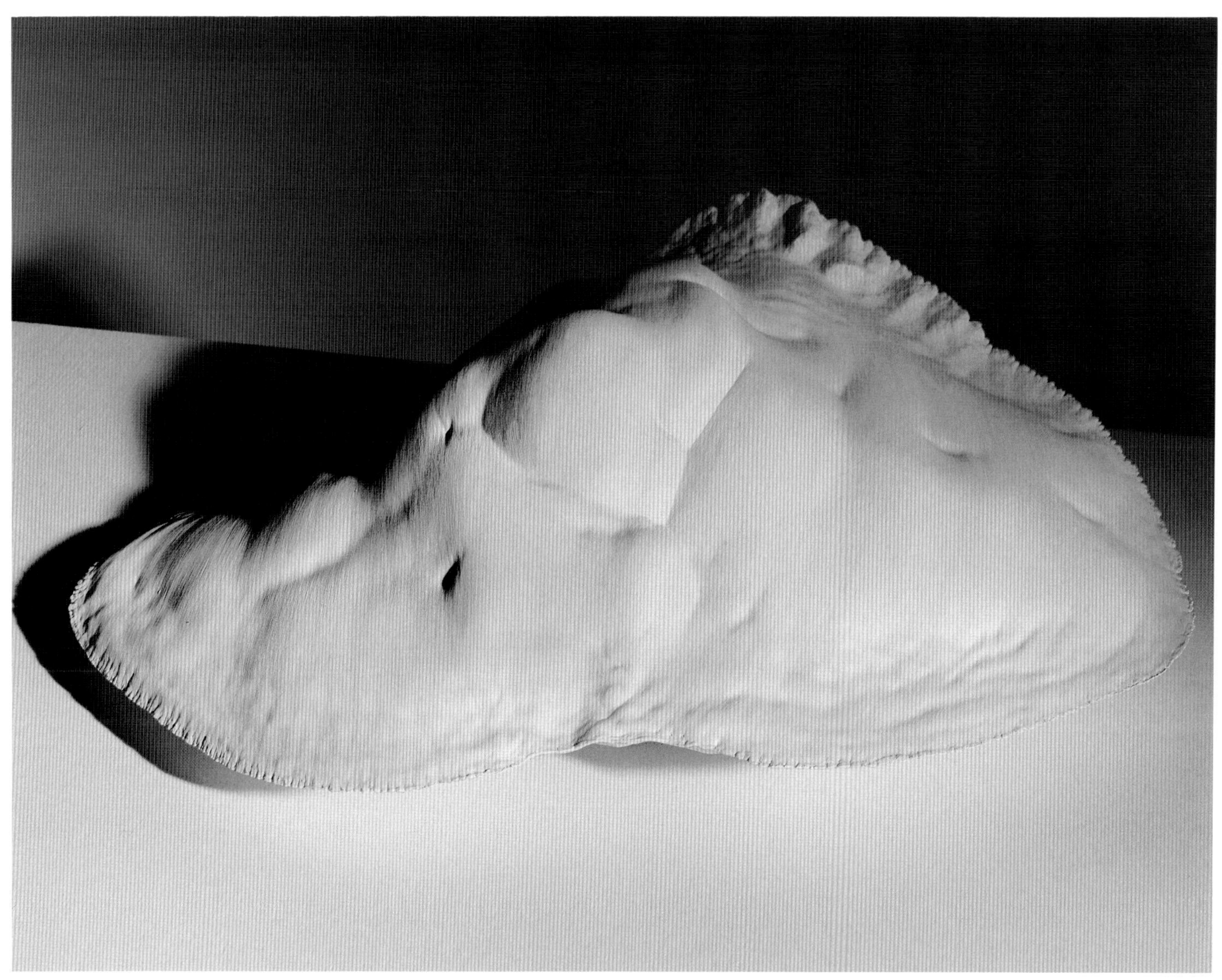

XI

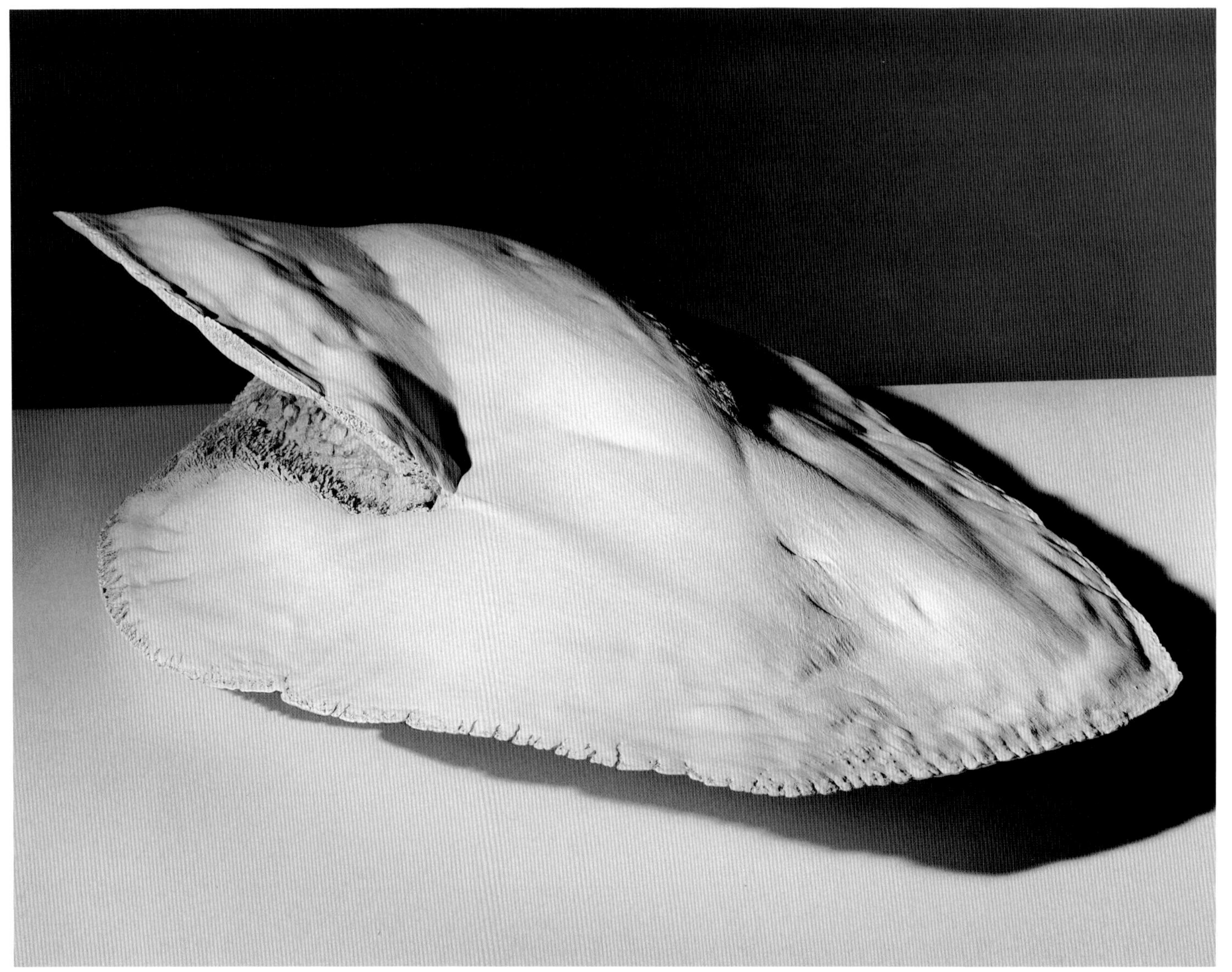

XII

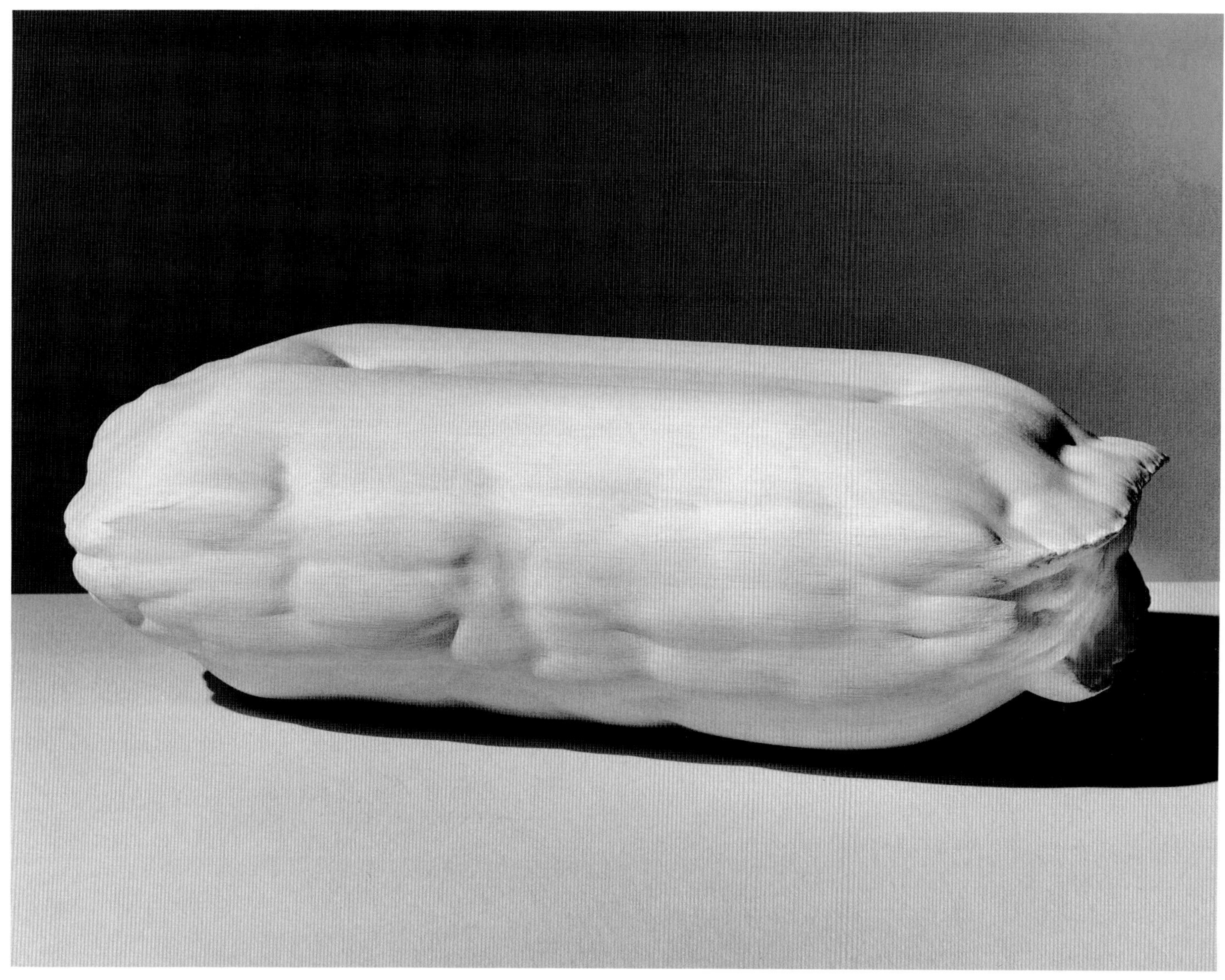

XIII

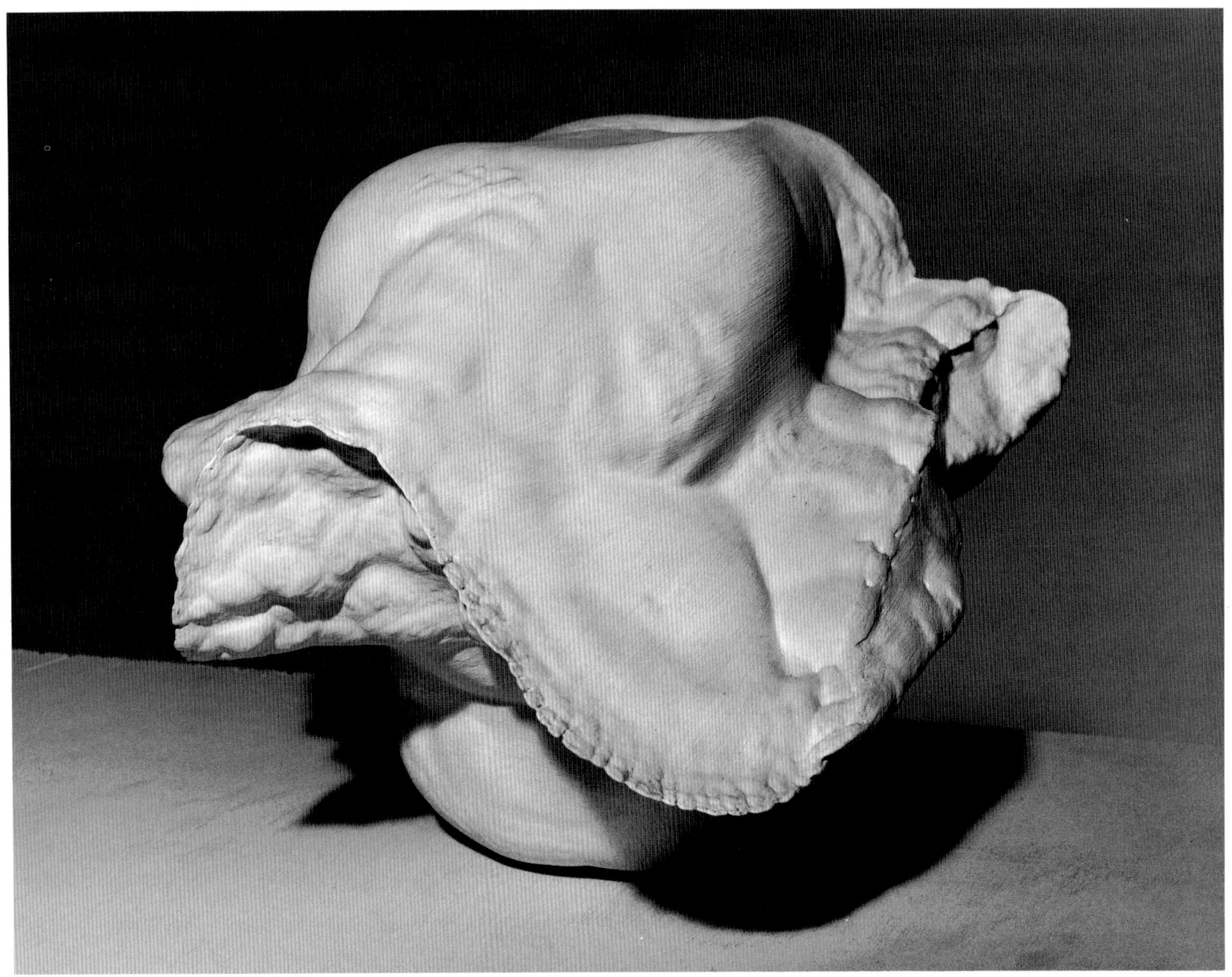

XIV

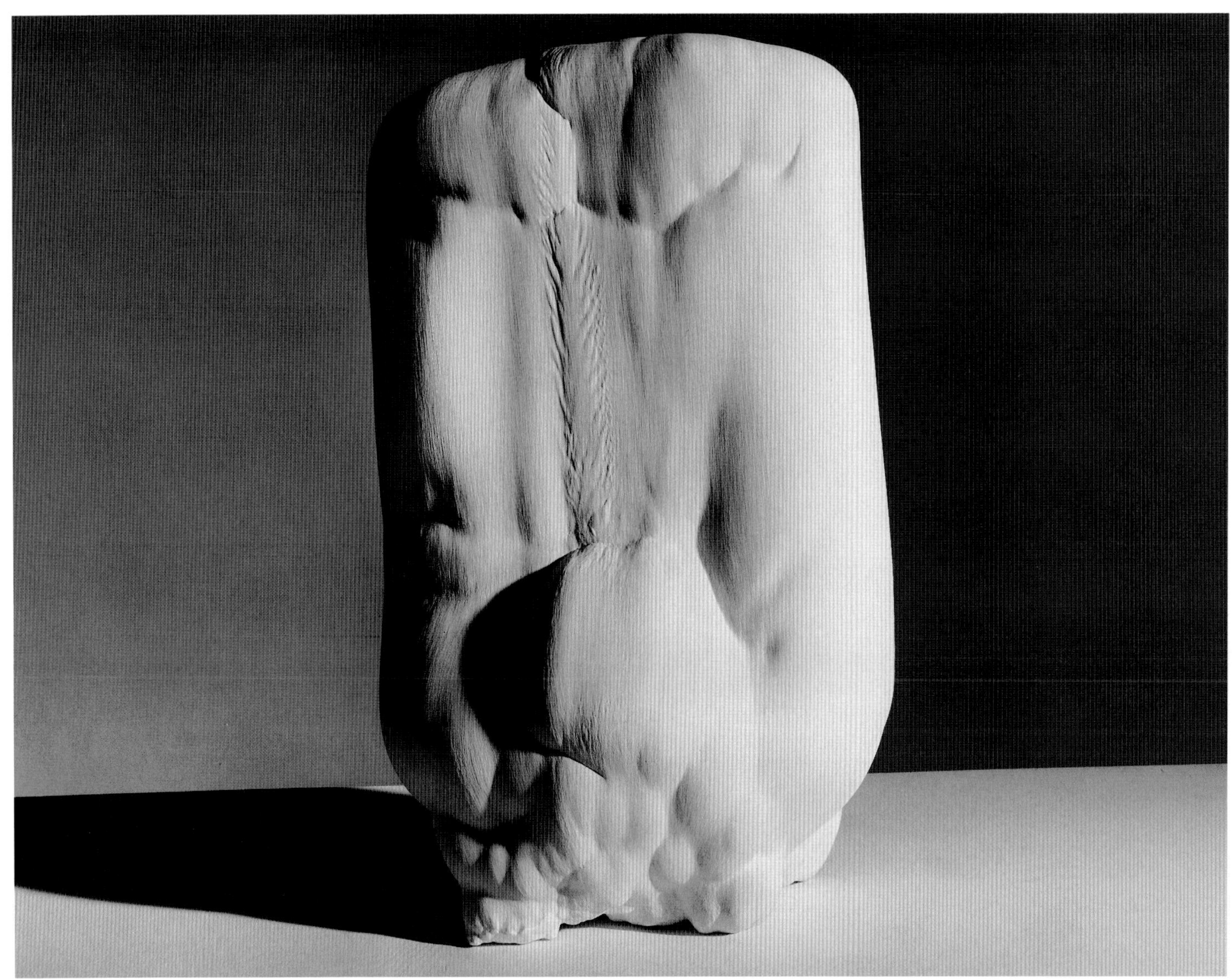

XV

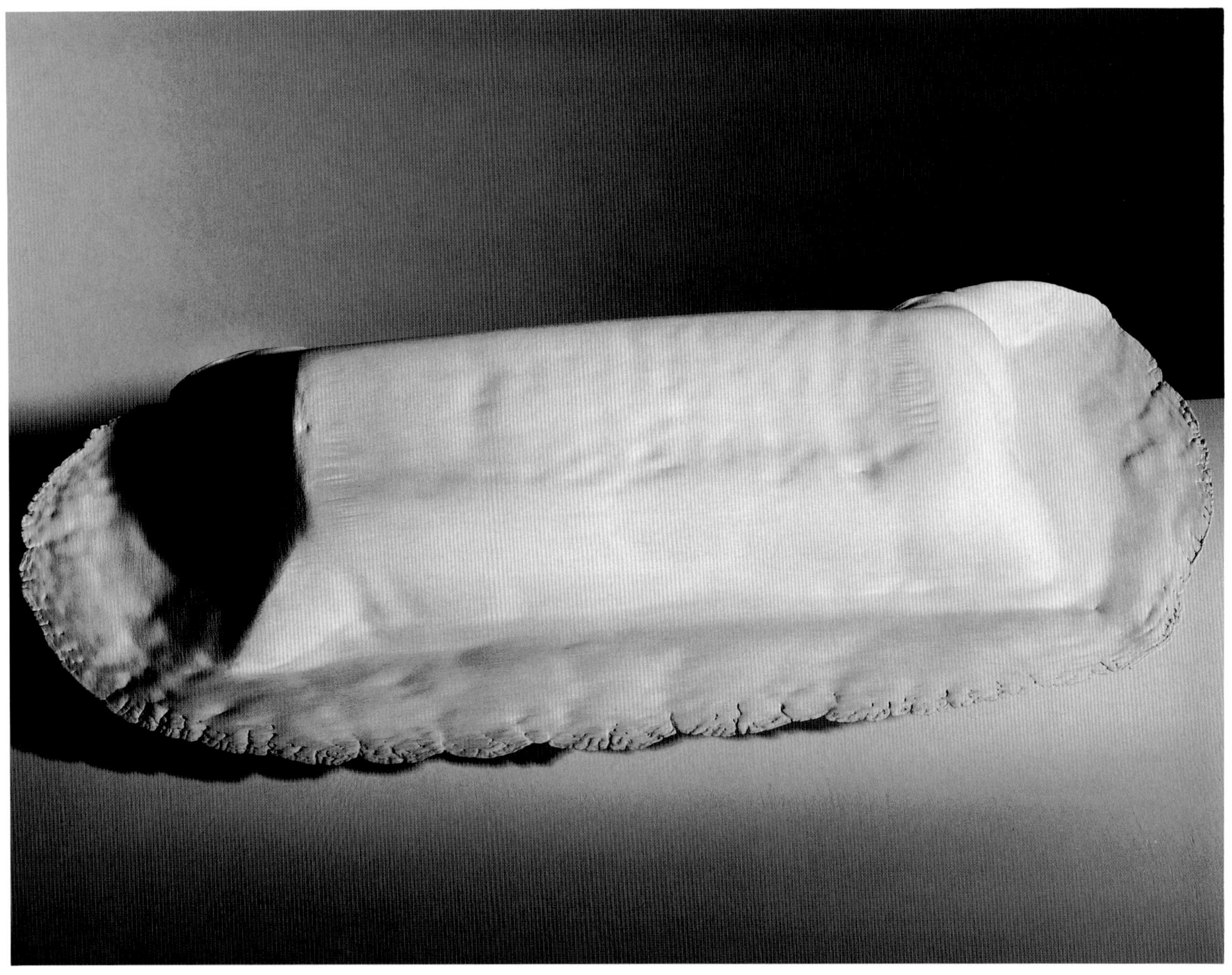

XVI

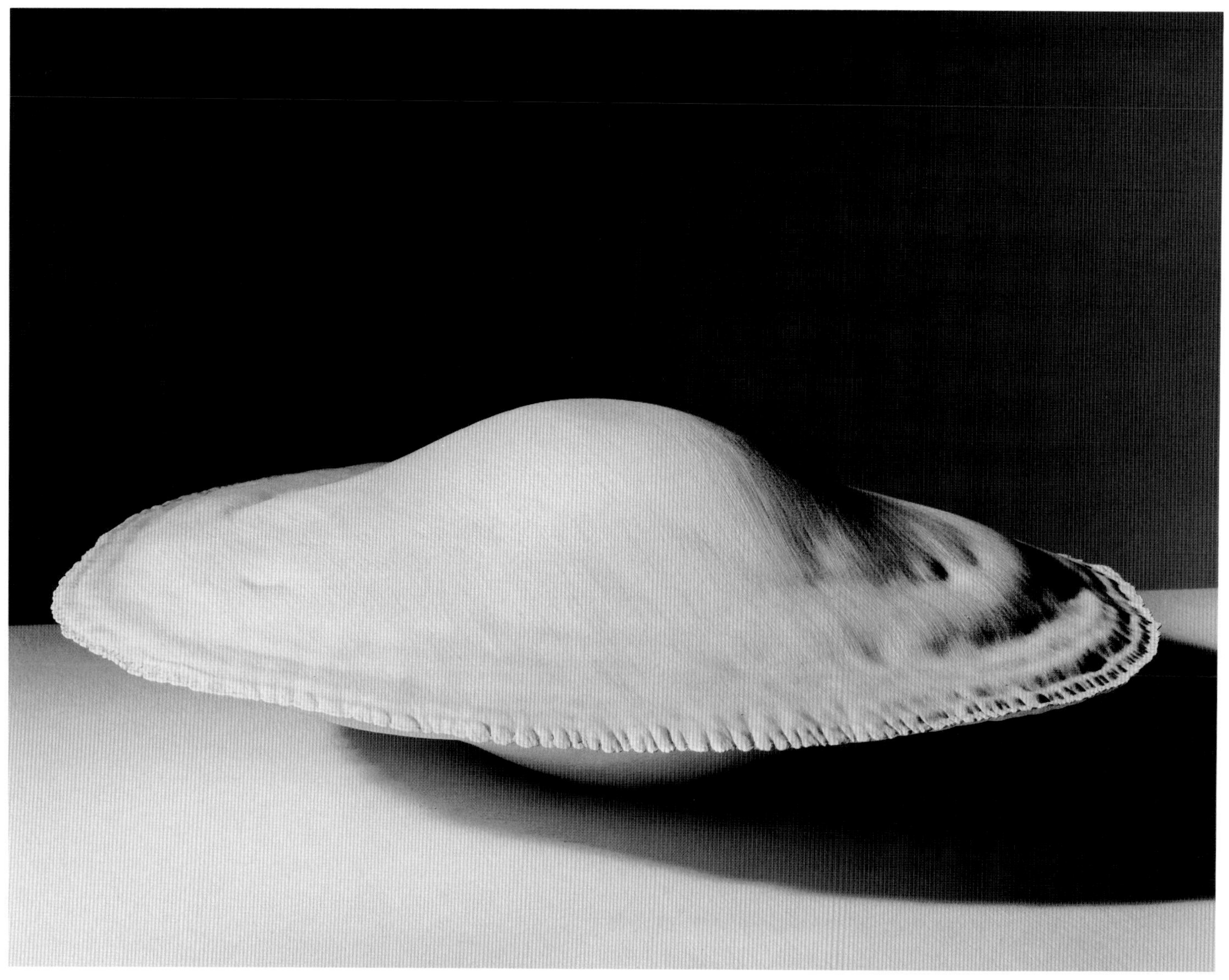

XVII

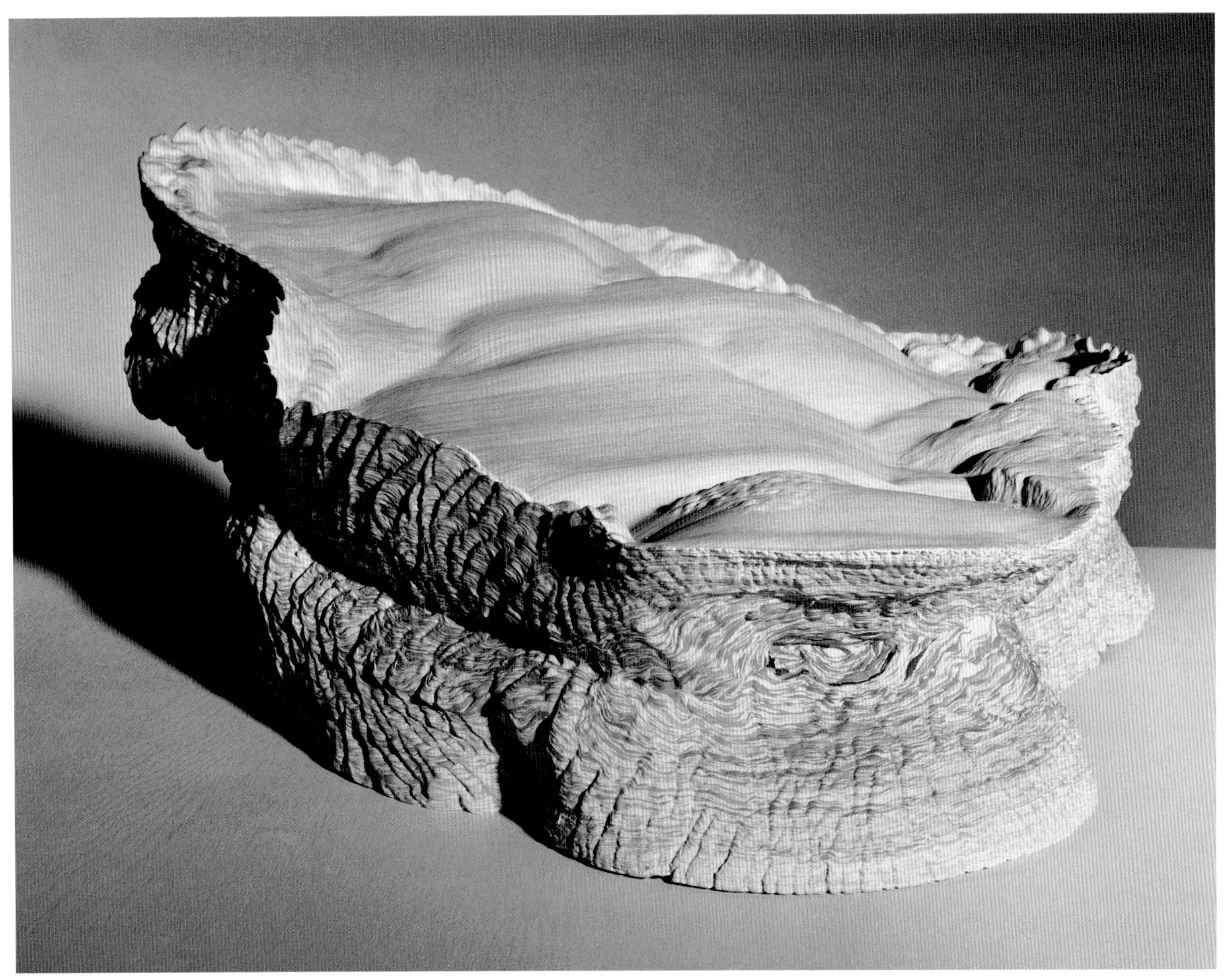

XVIII

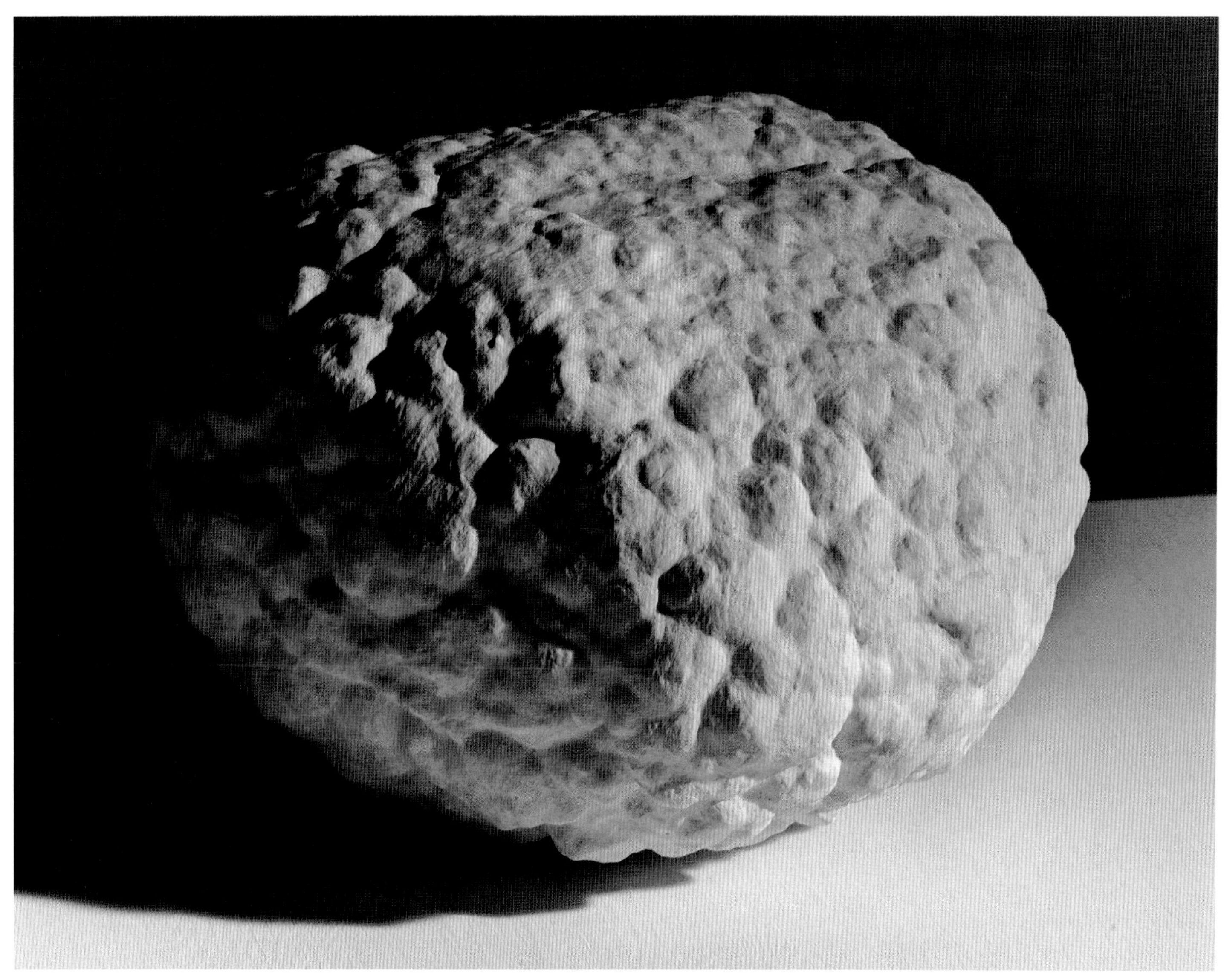

XIX

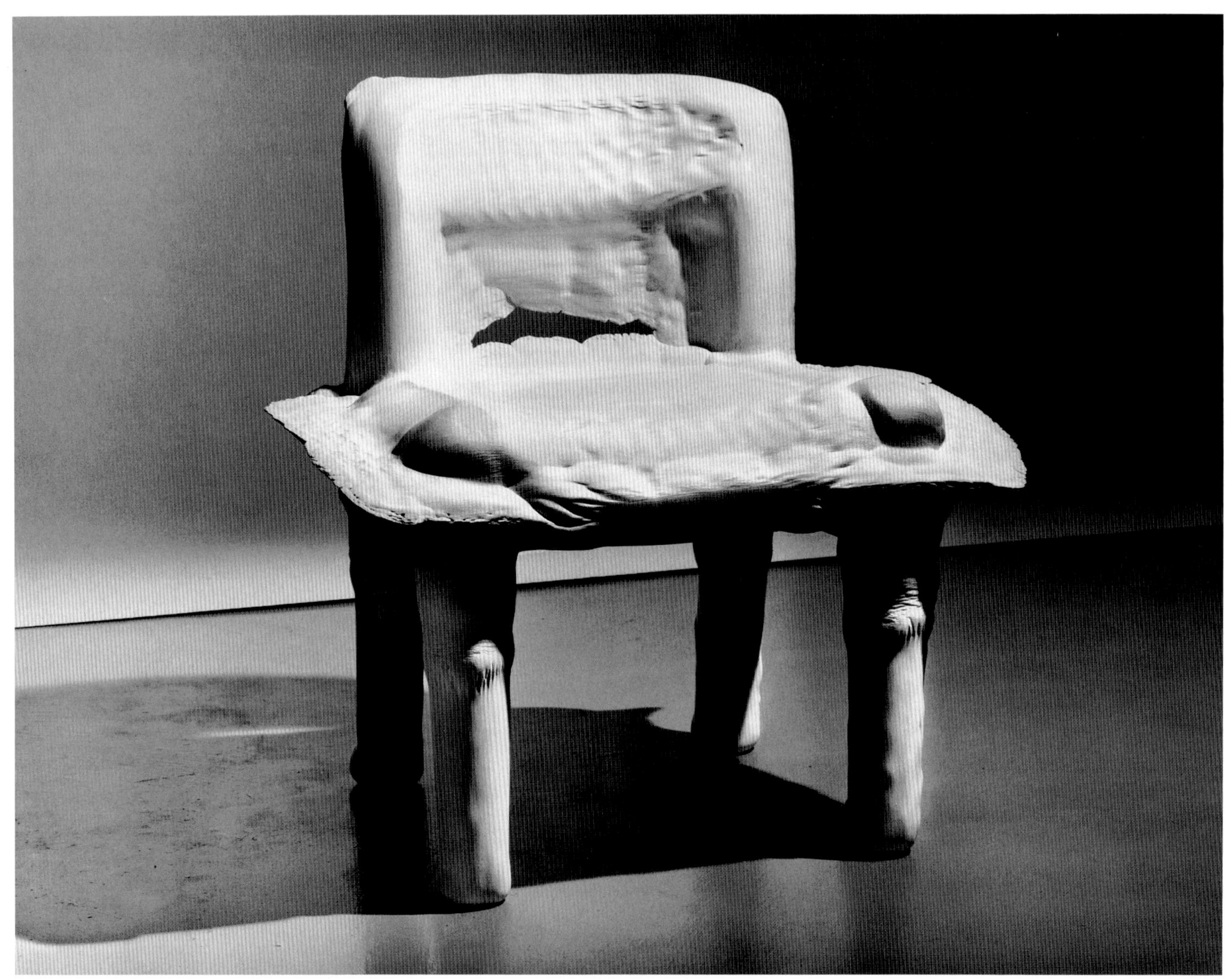

XX

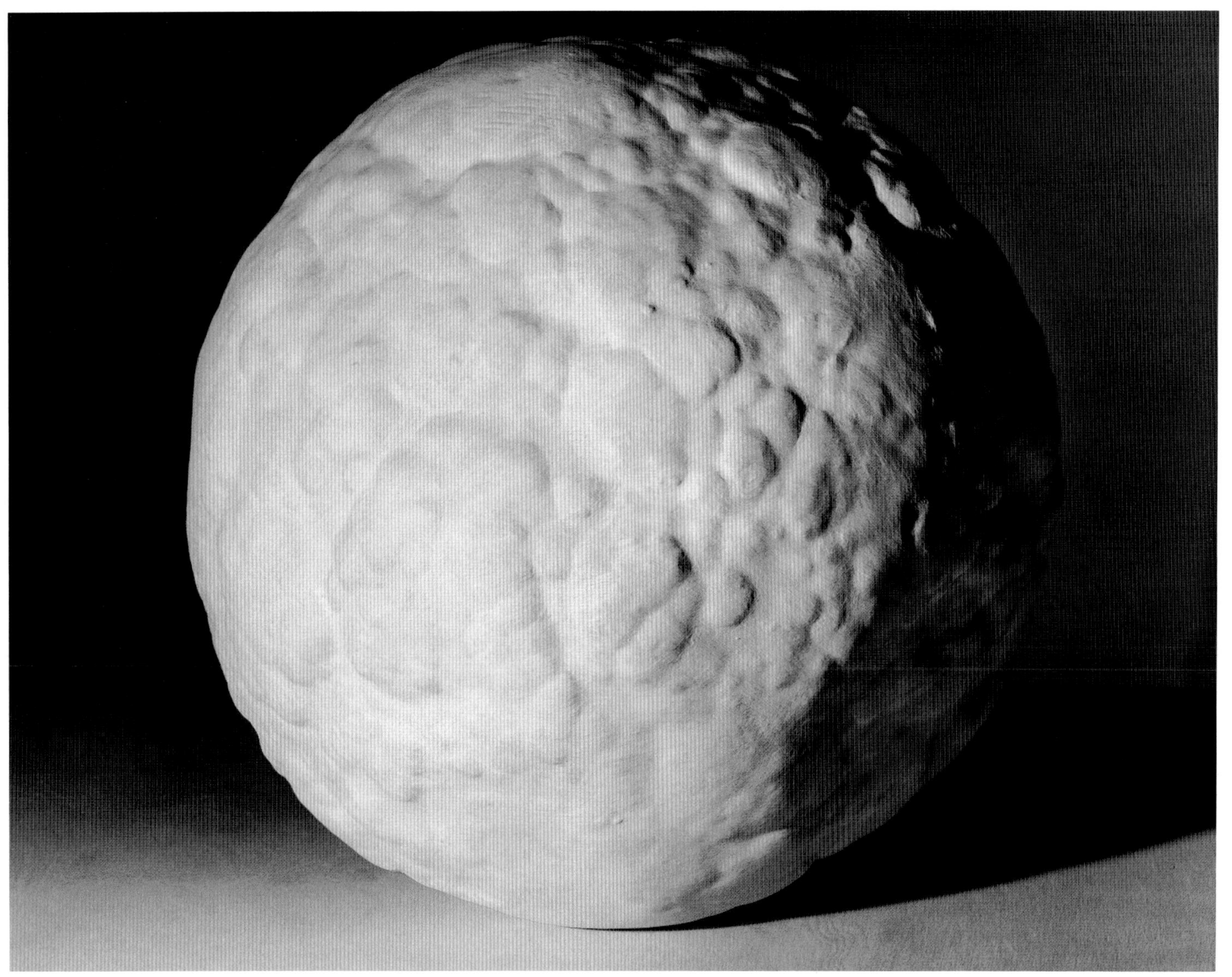

XXI

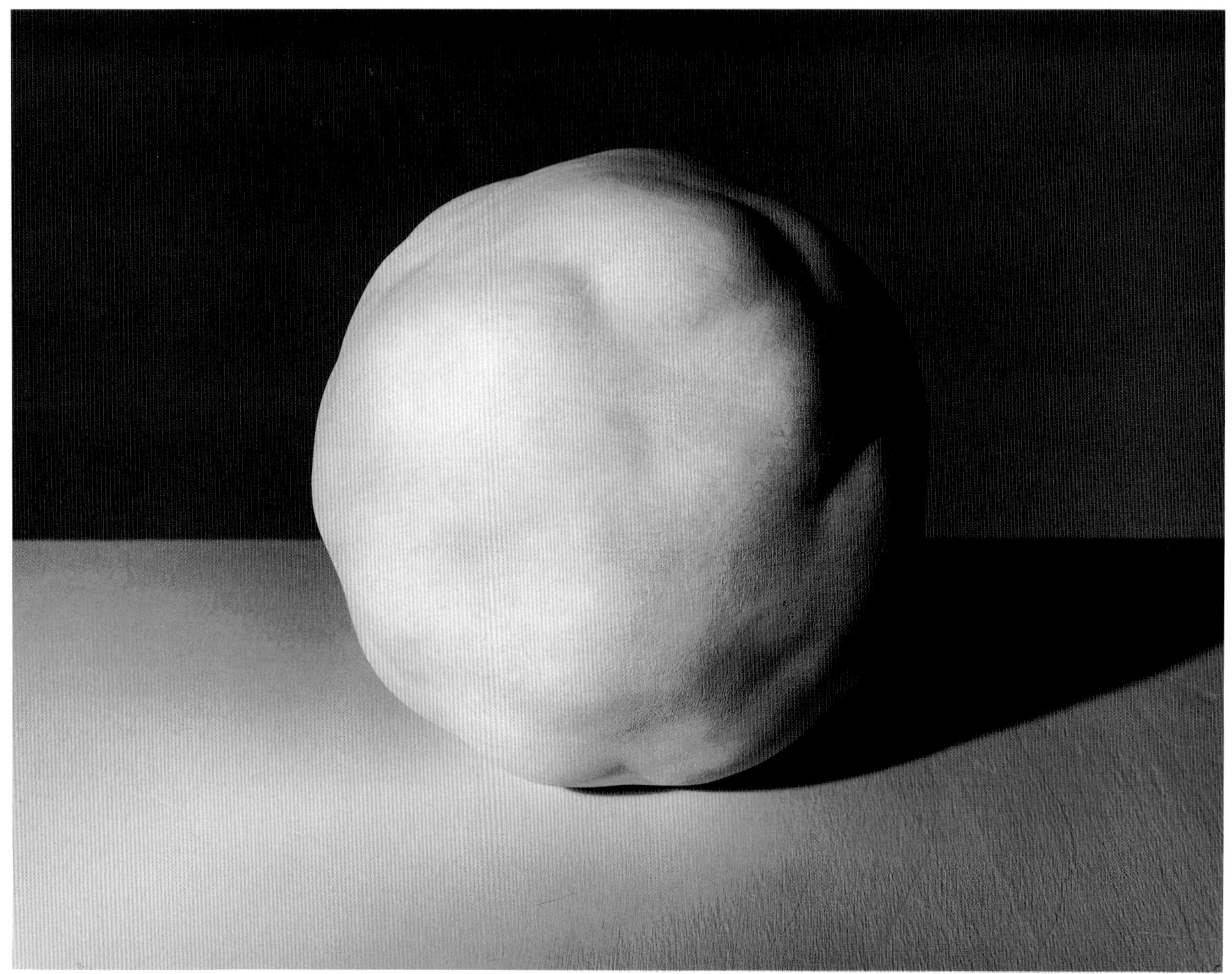

XXII

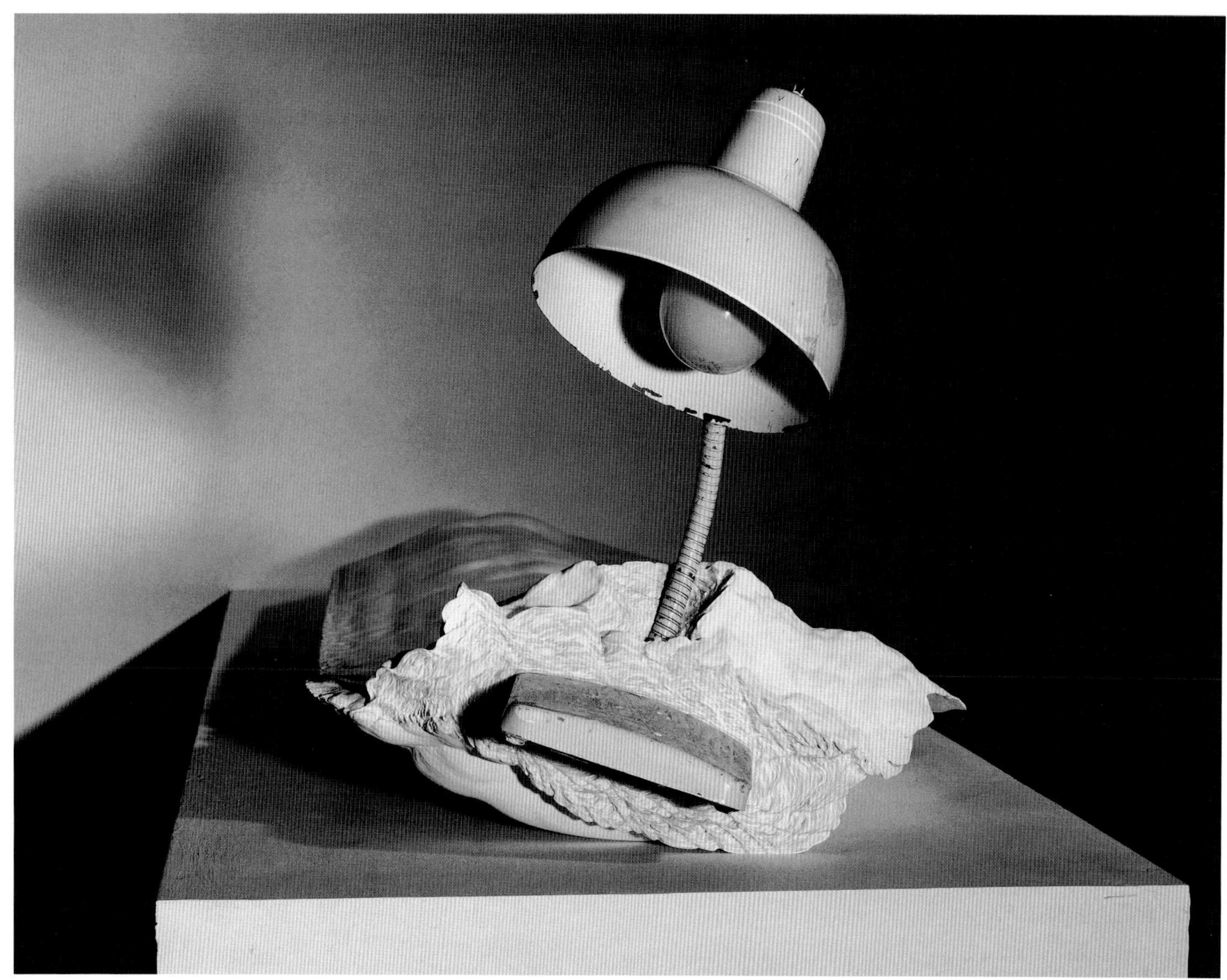

XXIII

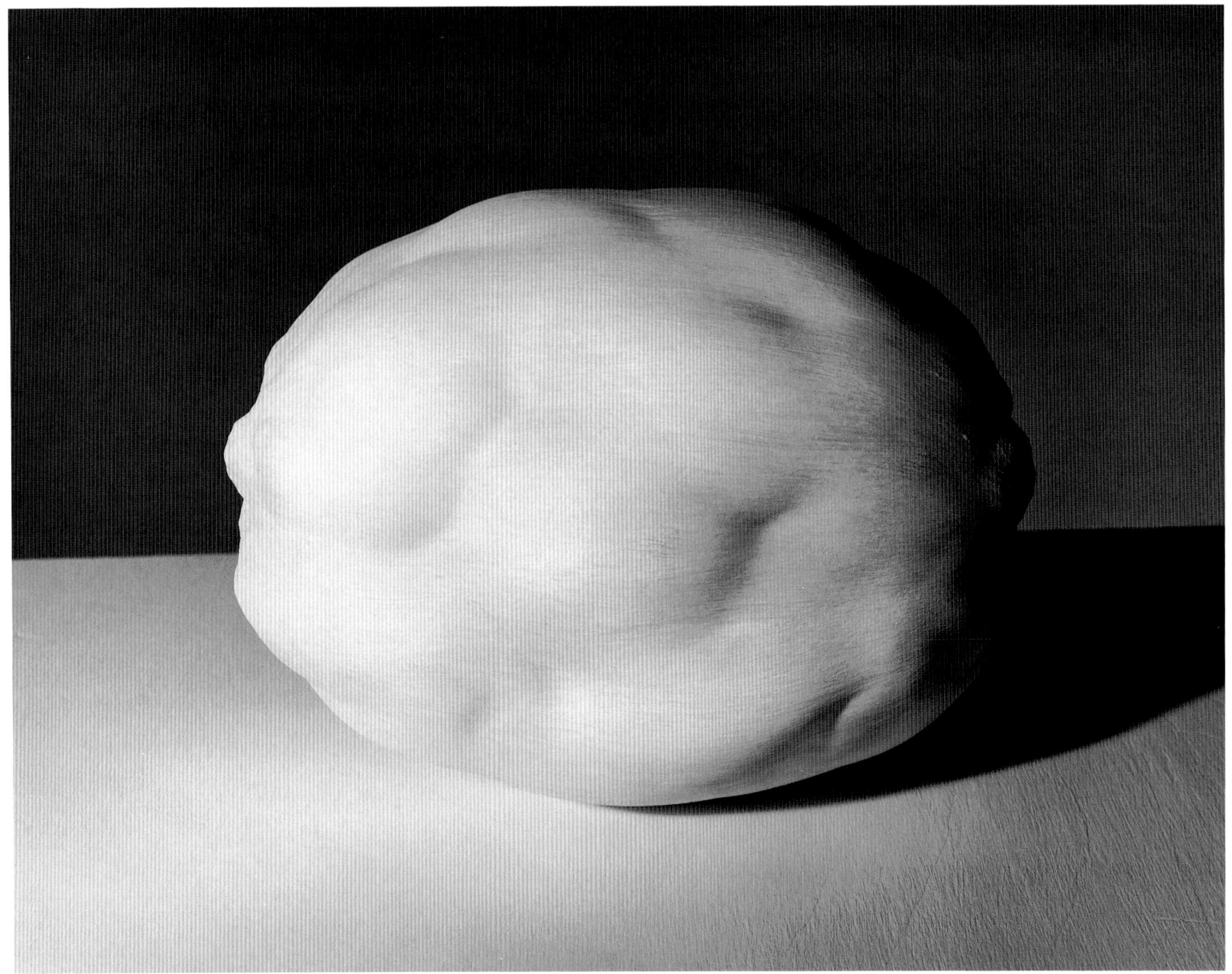

XXIV

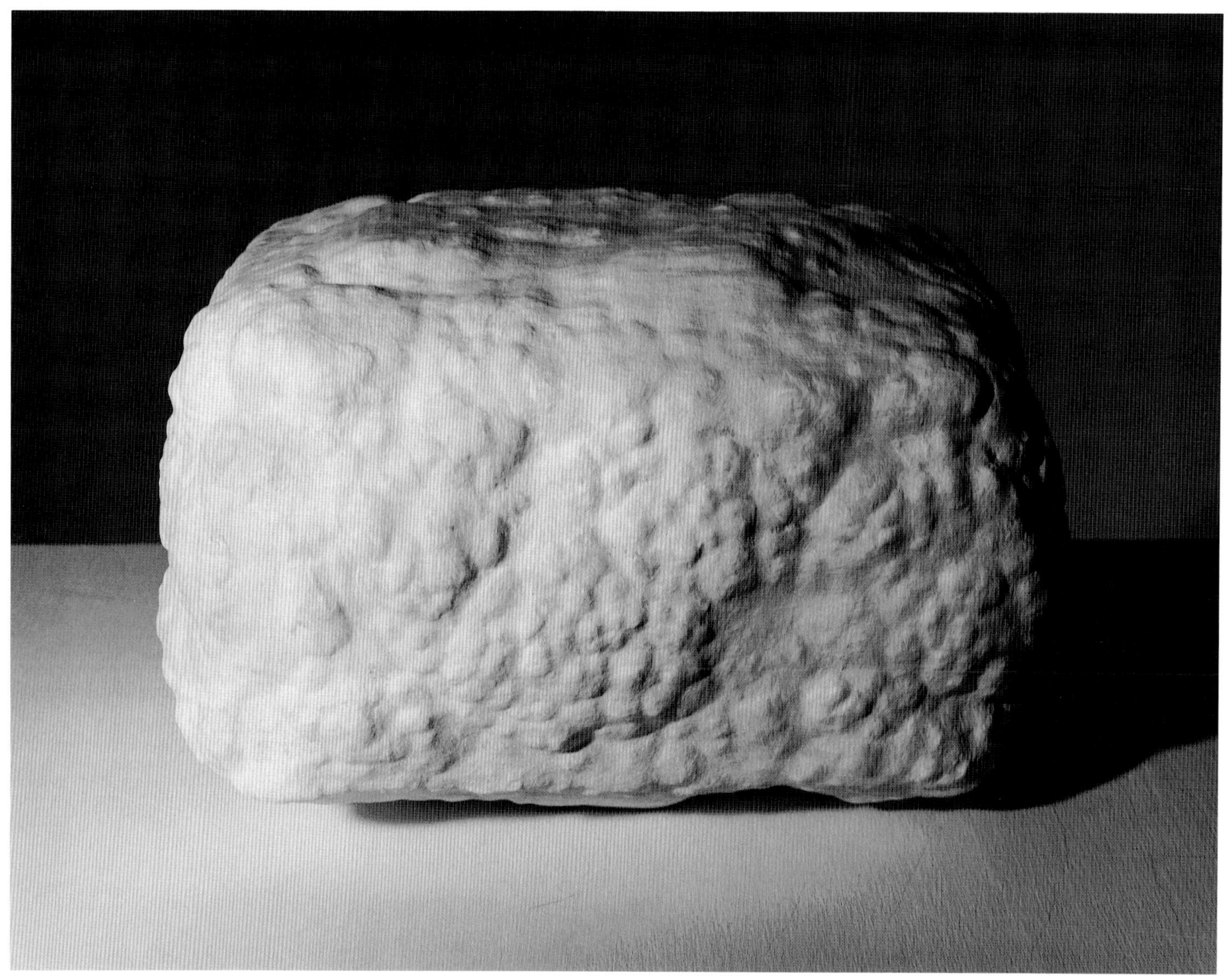

XXV

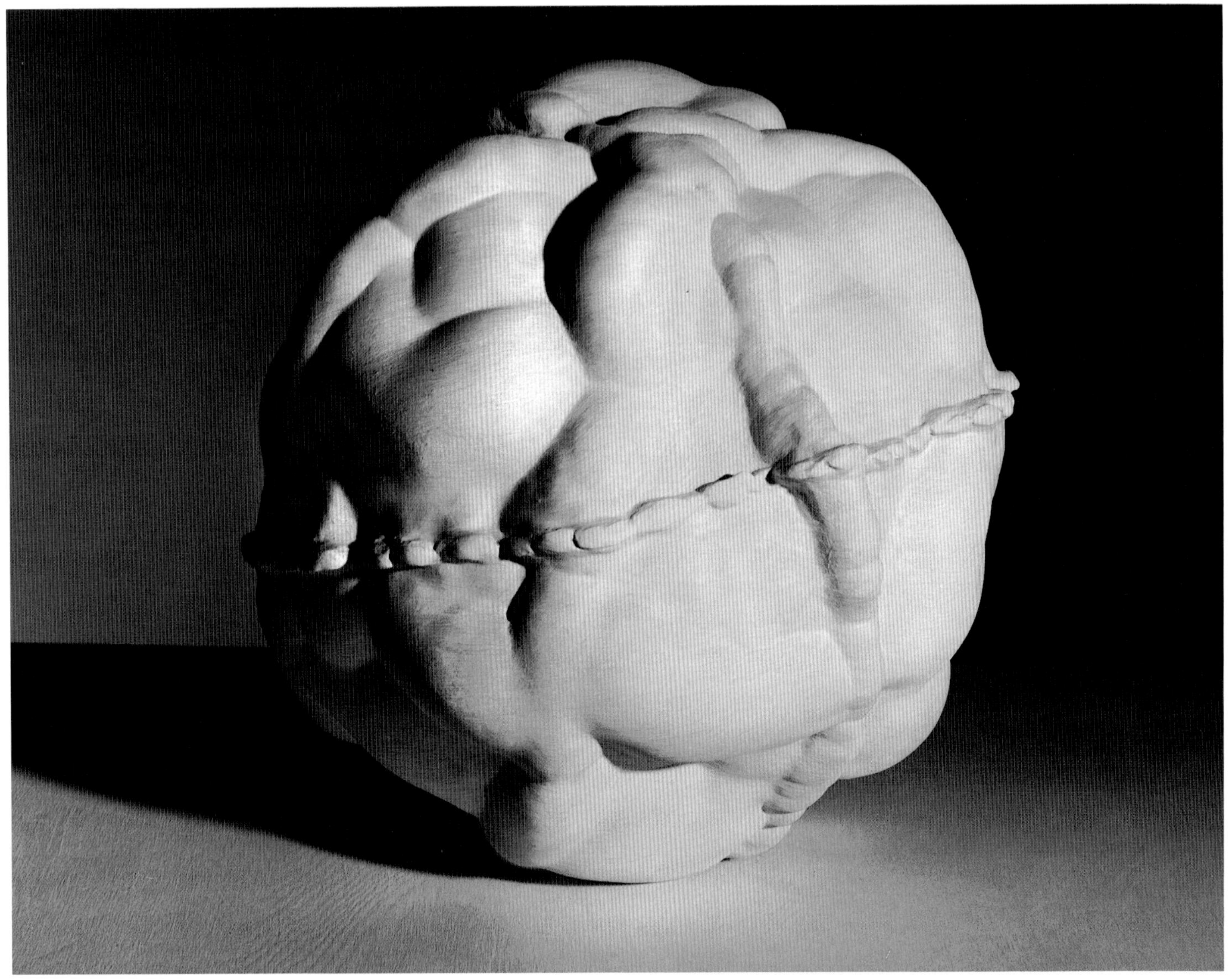

XXVI

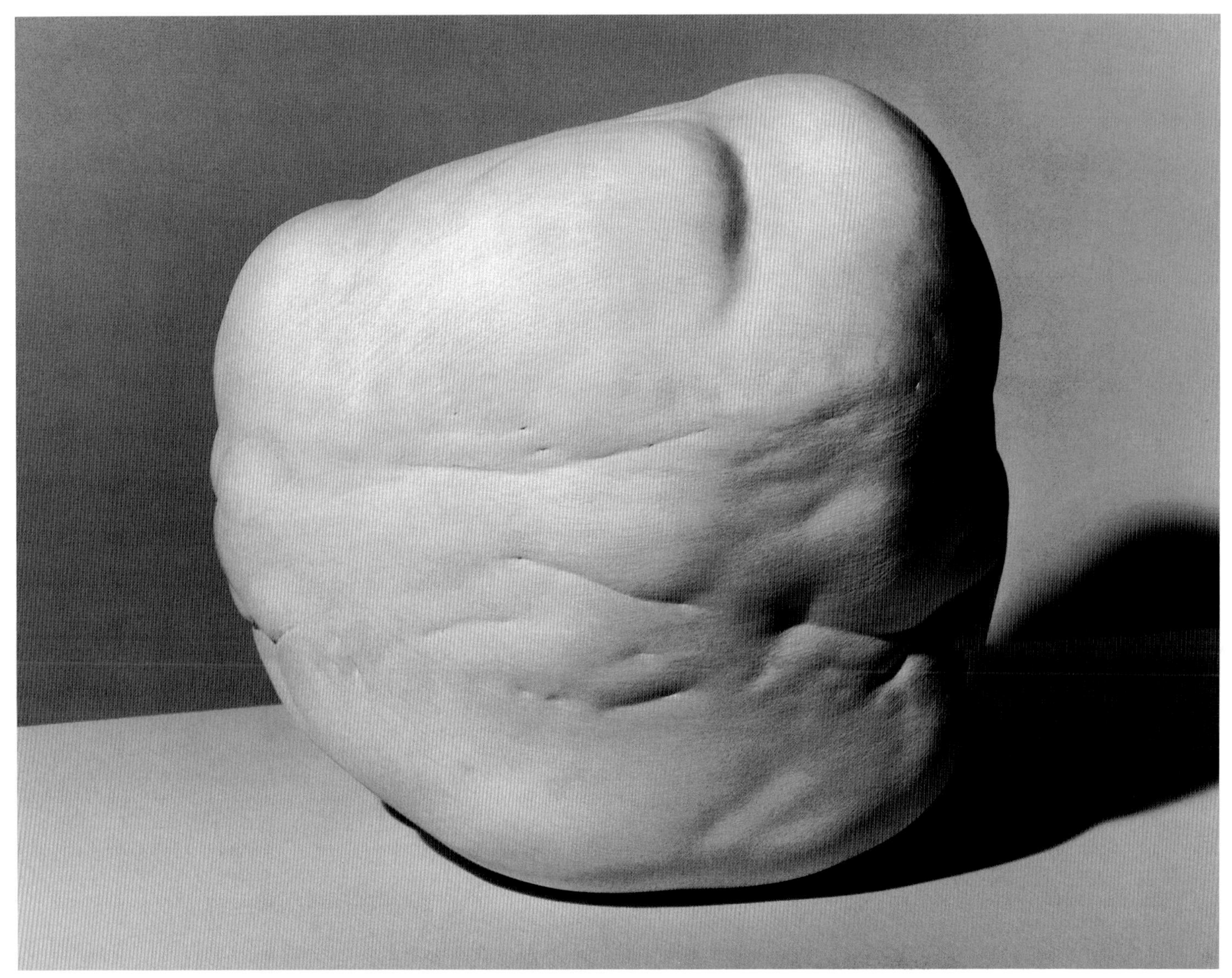

XXVII